exeter & devon arts centre

EXETER POETRY PRIZE 1996

ANTHOLOGY

ODYSSEY PRESS

ODYSSEY PRESS
Coleridge Cottage
Nether Stowey
Somerset

in association with
EXETER & DEVON ARTS CENTRE
Bradninch Place
Gandy Street
Exeter
Devon

ISBN 1 897654 89 8

CONTENTS

PREFACE

It is probably unsurprising that I have become a great fan of open poetry competitions such as ours, to which people locally and from all over the world respond. It's fascinating to watch this completely anonymous process lift work that, in poetry's great tradition, takes on complex issues, unfailingly uncovers the work of known poets daring to take their chance, and discovers exciting new voices.

My admiration and thanks to the Judges, Selima Hill, John Daniel and Derrick Woolf who present this Anthology as the conclusion of the 1996 Exeter Poetry Prize, and many who filled the criteria above will not know how close they came to the last shortlist. I would like to think that an Anthology such as this, giving so vivid a picture of the competition, will become an integral part of the Prize.

The impetus for launching this Prize is something for which I should thank Stephen Sims, Anne Born, Sandra Tappenden and Peter Faulkner, in addition to Odyssey Editor Derrick Woolf, all of whom are valued Literature advisors. The interest in the Prize in Exeter, around Devon, and further afield, is something we hope enables this Anthology to reflect both a national and regional picture, and I look forward eagerly to next year. Enjoy your reading.

Andy Morley
Arts Manager
Exeter & Devon Arts Centre

JUDGE'S REPORT

First of all how. People seem to want to know.

Well, I kept a few weeks clear, or as clear as I could, in my diary, and when Andy Morley delivered the boxes of poems, I put them in my end room, where my puppy would not shred them prematurely, and set to. I read them in batches of 100, aiming to extract approximately one in every four or five, aiming for twenty in every hundred. I had three boxes, **"no sorry"** (the largest, I have to say), **"maybe"** and **"yes"**. These filled up as the days went by. Before beginning each batch of a hundred or so, I re-read the "yes's" and the "maybe's" to reject them, if possible (I'm a soft touch), and to remind myself of the standard. I needed a shortlist of about 200 to bring forward to my fellow-judges.

What was I looking for? Hard to tell. I just know when a poem is alive and when it's dead. I apply a sort of mirror to it to see if it's breathing. I can tell you what I did not want to find: flagrant disregard for detail, panic-stricken endings that go nowhere, posey titles for undeserving poems, waffle, muddle and poems about grandfathers, which latter had to be really special to stand out, as, indeed, one did.

Other popular themes were, I am afraid to say, Dunblane; childhood (with or without the grandparents); alienation in a world of machines; despair in a world of destruction and disregard of nature; male violence.

Ironically, when the partner was at home, the poem was about hating him or her, when the partner was absent the poem was a poem of great love for them. Loss was by far the commonest theme. ***What is poetry for?*** I asked myself.The poems that reached the short-list were poems that spoke to me as if they meant it, as if they mattered, as if they wanted me to listen. As if it was their right to be there. And they were enjoying themselves - as poems, I mean, regardless of whether the subject-matter was heavy or light. I was looking for poems of passion, courage, vigilance, innocence, bloody mindedness. Poems that were out there doing their thing. Poems of quickness, lightness, exactitude, suppleness, surprise. Don't give me dreams and dolphins.

When the three judges' short-lists were brought together, I was surprised and delighted that about half the top 40 poems appeared on all three lists. These were briefly reassessed and went forward to form the basis of the winning list. We then fought for another six hours in the dark confines of the Arts Centre's Cabaret Theatre to come up with the remaining 20 recommendations and four winners.

There was one writer I would have died for. And I intended to bully the others into agreeing with me, whatever it took. Luckily for them, four poems of this entrant were mentioned in all our short short-lists, namely our top 40 favourites out of my short-list of 200. I wanted this writer to scoop all three prizes but was sensibly dissuaded.

To **Dancing With Bruno**, our congratulations.

The second prize winner was also a multiple entrant, both of whose poems were up there in the top ten (not much room up there when you consider that four places, at this stage, were already taken by Bruno and his gang). Derrick said **Grand Canyon** had "the tone of a serious poem". I couldn't have agreed more, but did feel that he and John were being hood-winked into thinking that therefore it *was* a serious poem, a seriously good poem. I preferred **Blood Orange** with its flashier images and more sparing way with the dreaded "concepts". However, thatsweep of fresh air in the middle of "Grand Canyon" sold it to me: *"I think I've gotten the myth/wrong again"*. A very winning tone, especially after all that rock bedding and pelvic flare. **The House Of Shattering Light**, again, was short-listed by us all. How could we not remember it? We weren't sure, and still aren't, what *"marin country"* is exactly, but one trusted the voice so much, it only made it more intriguing. With the grand high-vaulting ambitiousness of "Grand Canyon" and the irresistible confiding tone of "Dancing With Bruno" *("it is about love and work and tears and opportunity / I speak. It is about retreats and meanings and capturing time / I refer. It is about our head waiter who has been spied / by some of us riding away from the hotel with his dark / red jumper on ...")*, with these two, we thought the careful mystery of "The House Of Shattering Light" made a perfect winning three-some we were well satisfied with.

The Express and Echo Award was a battle between **In This House On This Morning**, which one judge in particular felt was a 'clear winner', and **The Casts We Both Forgot**, a well-behaved, well sustained, capable poem, we felt would be the popular choice. **Pass-Notes"** we commend very highly, with its rage - but so well orchestrated - against examinations, and the *"women in ginger slippers"* who patrol their halls.

Tuell Cross was short, possibly slight, but wouldn't go away. Strange, as the three judges were coming from very different places. But, whatever our subjective likes and dislikes, we knew a good poem when we saw one. "Tuell Cross" is a delight, with a light touch that is surprisingly difficult to master - if 'master' is the right word.

The Field-Guide to the Birds of Britain and Europe was another multiple entrant. In fact, one judge wanted this entrant, with another poem, **Rowing Grandma**, to win the whole thing. However we agreed in the end that, although worthy and reliable poems, they did not quite go far enough. But it is obvious the writer can write. So thank you for these spacious, inventive, human and enjoyable poems.

Crayfish was another poem which got three votes - a busy, happy poem with lots going for it. I liked the *'tame wild pig'* listening to Dvorak; the *"single severed hand"* applauding in the water.

We hope the recommendations will reflect the wide range and style of the entries. This was uppermost in our minds when we were considering poems for this category. Here was a chance for the quieter poem, such as **Encounter** and **Foxes**; the quirkier, such as **The Gender of Words**, and for the simple, moving poem, such as **Still Birth** and **Homes.** For the poem that got only one vote, but a very persistent one, such as **Rowing Grandma, Marching Season In Belfast, The Flood**, and, most controversial of all, **Visitant.** And for poems which, while not a popular choice, maybe were too efficiently literary to be ignored, such as **Through The Blue Door, A Sense of Place**, and not forgetting the highly effective **The Terrors and Mr. Peter**, and **Beethoven Has Been** from the creator of the prize-winning Bruno.

Perhaps the hardest thing to represent is the humour. But we did not want you to think we were at hospital bedsides *all* the time. We hope **Seducing The Lead Swan** will bring a smile to your lips – it was certainly my favourite title! – also **Dangling Participle, In This House On This Morning, Elizabeth Reflects.**

As for the rest, there is a lot of eroticism about. Most of it had to go, but the pushy 'pig-jawed' **Visitant** insisted on a place. Of course, love and sex is the great theme of poetry, the easiest to write about badly, and the hardest to write about well. I therefore commend to you – we were impressed – the poems **My Son Is Beautiful As The Sun** which is weird and wonderful and must be about love, if not sex, in its own wild way. Also **The Letter**, a heart breaking story it's hard to forget; **Pleasure Places** which include not only *"the master bedroom of the Wimpey Show Home"* and *"the toilet of BA 012"* but a place *"where no language exists, gone from where we rest"*, **Milk Powder**, and lastly, **Spoons** – reading a sensitive portrayal of love-making is a pleasure. Finally, four personal favourites – for their thoughtfulness and beauty, I recommend **Fish, Between Ourselves, Epiphany Eve** and **Company.**

Thank you for all the poems. We know that we have been as fair and attentive as we could have been – and trust our final choices meet with your approval.

We got surprisingly involved with all the nameless writers and their many hopeful poems, and, in spite of the hard work (or is it because of it?) feel a sense of loneliness as they disappear again. We look forward to finding out who everyone is – they were judged, of course, anonymously.

Finally, we would like to thank Andy and Maria and all those members of their staff who helped organise the *most-well-organised poetry competition* in England. It must be. And it was a great pleasure to be one of this year's judges.

Selima Hill
Exeter, October 1996

WINNING POEMS

FIRST PRIZE

david grubb

DANCING WITH BRUNO

Bellagio, Italy

When they have drifted into the dining room
and been shown to their tables, when they have taken
the opportunity to identify people at other tables
by those signals and associations of etiquette, when
the view onto the lake has again been consumed and
comparisons made with yesterday or last year or many
moons ago as if the stage set had shifted slightly,
when the wine and the water and five courses have been taken
and the contours of the lake have indeed expanded but
chiefly due to the wine and the very strong local cheese,
and then the period of simply staring out at the lake,
and then the decisions whether or not to stroll or to take
coffee or more simply to return to a room of cool dreams,
when expressions of pleasure and gratitude have been expressed
and the lifts to Reception or the roof garden or floors two to
five have made their distance, when the dinner things have
mysteriously become the breakfast things,
the waiters and waitresses, the cooks and their assistants begin to
make their journeys into the late evening green,
to those houses we may have passed by, to those clubs
we chose to ignore, to rooms with different views and other
conversations. It is about love and work and tears and opportunity
I speak. It is about retreats and meanings and capturing time
I refer. It is about our head waiter who has been spied
by some of us riding away from the hotel with his dark
red jumper on, the noise of his small motor cycle, the look
of relief on his countenance which is normally so bland,
and we begin to create another life for him and a wife who
will dance in front of him and cover her body in
moon and sing of cheeses that will bring him to
his feet. To dance with Bruno until breakfast time.

SECOND PRIZE

diana m sabot

GRAND CANYON

I never knew rock could look so soft,
cliffs bruised with sun, muted reds and pinks,
the mild, exposed colors
of flesh, though sometimes flesh
feels like rock, warm to the touch
but resistant. When he bears down on me
in my desert bed I think how hard
we both are, how heavy. I can take his pressure
and he mine. This night is a canyon. Slow

as geologic time it forms, from rim to basin
rock bedding down with rock, hot and dry
our mouths, our lips of sand. Loosed after too much wine
his flat hands move my hips, our bones shift
deep beneath the skin, grind
in sockets worn smooth out of calcium, the pelvic flare
and ribcage kiss, knee pinning knee and hips
jammed together, plates of our foreheads –
two forces, one substance.

I think I've gotten the myth
wrong again. In another poem
there would be water – rain on the window
or the faucet leaking. When I remember
the Navajo story, it's the woman
who is liquid, the insistent dripping. She trickles
through cracks and ledges, works down
to the inner gorge drop by drop, small seep at the contact
of deep red shale with underlying slate. She is creek
and spring, moist earth, dark bubbling, a haven for mosses
clinging lush to wet walls. She leaves
fossil prints of ancient rains
spattered across the talus slopes, she feeds mesquite

and catclaw, tamarisk and tumbleweed,
camelthorn, desert almond, seep willow
and arrowweed. In the basin she roils
brown and wild between rock walls, unleashed
like a freight train, roaring froth and swirl.

And if he is limestone, siltstone,
the sandstone that will crumble in a hand,
slab after soft slab, she cuts through him. This was the creation.
Two forces locked in one empty landscape,
plateau rising up, river bearing down, water and rock caught
in an embrace so fierce, it wore
a gaping hole into the earth.

THIRD PRIZE

pascale petit

THE HOUSE OF SHATTERING LIGHT

We house-hunted in marin country.
I was weak, so you fed me the hearts of deer.

Just beyond the dunes and before the scrub
we found the house of our dreams --

walls that retreated according to the moon,
floors that sprouted thorns when we quarrelled.

We discovered a secret room
where children were preparing themselves.

Some took out their eyes.
Some took off their noses, ears or legs
while some broke themselves exactly in half.

That night your snores quietened.
The truth butterflies flew out of your mouth.
My sweat pricked me like tiny needles,

my skin glowed with body lights.
I could see into my interior
as if gazing at a starry night.

I gathered the sweat from my skin,
poured it into this bottle,
labelled it The House of Shattering Light.

When I am homesick, I open the stopper.
At first, I smell a girl
with the heart of a deer.

When the blood–smell fades,
then, the waves of marin country
bring me the eyes, ears and legs of my babies.

THE EXPRESS & ECHO AWARD

alan peacock

THE CASTS WE BOTH FORGOT

When I was twelve, he taught me to tie flies:
how to rib the body, wax the silk,
strip and twist a hackle to make legs.

He explained the gape and bend of a down–eyed hook,
the use of hackle–pliers; talked me through
the tricky whip–finish, to varnishing the head.

He left me, in this language, all he knew:
an urge for rivers, at dawn and after dark,
the pluck and splash that tell a fish's size,

the subtleties of seasons; and at home,
the colour–plates in Hardy's Angler's Guide,
icons whose names had the rhythm of how he cast.

His coaching grooved the fly–rod's lift and pause,
my action modelled on the turn of his wrist.
But the act is incomplete. What have I missed?

The next rise fades downstream: I wade deep
to a likely run, listening for what he'd say,
for ideas which ripple, glint, and die away ...

The pool skitters with flies we both could name,
yet I still cannot make contact with his eyes,
and don't know if he ever felt the same

about home, work, love, or being alone.
A shiver of breeze riffles the ash–leaf calm;
my shoulder never felt the hug of his arm.

Spasms of anger made his veins stand out,
frustration with angina left him drained.
Shadows emerged, but never words, of doubt:

self-taught in everything, unrecognised,
weighing his long-accumulated pain,
he knew he would never see us both again,

as we stood there, on the path, before we left:
his face turned sideways, silent yet bereft.
I sort through tackle-boxes, just to look

in old tobacco-tins at feathers and hooks,
the kinked and tangled casts we both forgot.
Could they still teach me to untie this knot?

HIGHLY COMMENDED

christopher burchell

TUELL CROSS

The sun was a six inch
Blood red plate
One inch above the horizon,
Hanging over Mr. Alford's
Recently served sow.

As we walked the lane,
The small square field
Was grey green in the dusk,
And Mrs. Barden's cat
Slunk charcoal near Diane's.

diana m sabot

BLOOD ORANGE

The night the moon turned to rust
we opened all our doors,
brought strangers to our kitchen
and danced in sheer dresses,
wanting it to change us, the planet's shadow
moving like a spread of iodine
over white skin, unbearably slow,
dulling the clean bright round
until midnight, when it crossed back again.
                    On my tongue
the taste of your lipstick, sweet and metallic,
on the windowsill, red tulips and milk:
you'd made me so beautiful
I couldn't speak all night,
and stayed close to the glass so the moon
could touch me, my cheeks cool and matte
with powder, my face a pearl
in the strange dim light. I couldn't
look at you when you did it,
when your hand drew my mouth
and widened my eyes, black kohl
on the lash-line, scarlet-filled lips.
In the morning his kisses
flowered on your neck like plums,
a little blood coaxed in whorls to the surface,
delicate as fingerprints,
startling as scars.
                    Dazed and unclean
we drank tea in the noon-light,
and I peeled an orange
with meticulous fingers
digging under the hard rind piece by piece
until the fruit was bare in its soft white skin.
I parted it to reveal the shock of crimson,
bright and unreal in the open air;

I put a section in my mouth and felt the color run everywhere.

david grubb

BEETHOVEN HAS BEEN

Beethoven has been in the woods all night.
He does not know that we know.
He is waiting for the snow, the rain, the thunderstorm
to end. He is waiting for the great light to become
again. He is waiting for the trees to stop dancing.
He is imagining that the great beasts that must
live there are universally bonded. Meanwhile the
dragonflies whiz about like exclamation marks,
he sits at the place where his piano might be
and mentally goes through the motions. His mind
fingers the inner reason of the galaxies and every
so often he is almost stunned by his own intuition.
When dawn arrives he will have completed his new
symphony. It will earn him some money and more time
and now he feels he will be able to handle all the interviews
and the charisma thing and be able to flash at the camera
that crazy grin. The meaning of music, the cascade of
art, the purpose of silences, the revelation of structures,
the jazzy bits, what the favourite colour is and the choice
of wine. Could he speak up? It's been a long time. The
wisdom of the symphonic form. Where does it all come from?
Beethoven has been in the woods all night. He does not
know that we know. He is not like the other men who go
there; writers, scientists, politicians, secret agents, gardeners
and architects. They all have a go at music, of course. It is
perhaps the only way. So many of them thought that there
would be something else, not of this world, but there you go.
In the woods there is that sense of terror about to be overcome
by the angels. The trees can be trusted. The why is out there
but far off. The basic instinct is to be creative and keep
the tune simple. Sometimes there is discussion about the meaning
of daylight but mostly there is this totality of expectation.
Beethoven has been in the expectation all night.
He has told me this and I am telling you but.

r moulson

THE FIELD GUIDE TO THE BIRDS OF BRITAIN AND EUROPE

The male great northern diver swims
motionless in its summer plumage
beside its double dressed for winter
on the same wave. *On breeding waters*
gives loud screams and yodels. And then
Maniacal laughter. Plate 1.

The albatross is steering clear
of mariners and such. The crow's
not doing anything disgusting.
While doves are listening for the obvious
rhyme, the grounded lark keeps stumm,
and swans are all reduced to scale.

There's a king but no queenfisher,
a night but not a dayingale,
many sparrows, one sparrowhawk,
three different bustards, one sole shag,
and a display of tits, mostly male,
blue, bearded, marsh coal, crested, great.

They all share the same piece of sky.
The red and black kites, the hen, marsh
and Montagu's harriers, the booted
eagle, the honey and common
buzzards fly up the page in perfect
formation, each with its markings.

Five hundred birds in full colour.
They fly auspiciously from right
to left. Or sit in puddles stuck
to their reflections. Or perch on twigs
detached from trees. Or, standing rapt,
their feet grip the white of paperspace.

bill greenwell

PASS NOTES

When I was a boy,
they waltzed me into the wall
of examinations. I was served

a worm of string,
and a slab of paranoid paper.
Women in ginger slippers

patrolled the hall,
skating the iron silence
with wide eyes in the sides

of wizened heads.
I huddled my limbs, and waited
for bells to ring which didn't:

instead, I poised my
special pen, steady and deaf
until they tidied my name away,

and turned me out.
I've led a fugitive existence, since:
no good, it seems, at being good.

To help my child,
I have made the front room a replica
of all examination halls.

To quell his nerves,
meals are invigilated. I watch
(as does my wife) the spoons pass

the test of his lip.
He has memorised the membrane
of every pea upon his plate.

james sutherland smith

CRAYFISH

On coarse grey paper with poster paints
A child has shaped a dark blue jointed creature
Which floats between verticals of weed and hints
Of river current in horizontal zig-zags.

"When I was a little girl I'd sit bare legged
On the wooden bridge and watch them swimming backwards.
Village boys would catch so many when they dragged
Their nets beneath the banks. We'd eat the tails.

Then there was the metal works and tannery
Which made the water tobacco-coloured.
Crayfish are fragile." This from Dana B-,
Delicate herself, who also describes

How in 1949 she and her twin brother,
Aged ten, were going to America,
But at the airport were turned back. Their mother
Couldn't bear to let them go without new clothes

And had delayed their flight a morth. A mistake.
The police cracked down. Their father, teacher
Of geometry and headmaster got the sack.
They were exiled to the village of the crayfish

And for a time they lived only in a hut.
Dana B- tells me of a tamed wild pig
Which would rest its muzzle on their feet
When they listened to Dvořak on the radio.

Dana B- walks backwards with a tray of coffee
Through a group of stouter, glossier colleagues.
How much do I know of crayfish biology?
Haemocyanin for oxygen, long feelers

Like slender twigs, animal and plant debris
For diet, the first to die from changes
In Ph or temperature and moving quickly
In the water, a single severed hand applauding.

"I'm sorry if I bore you with my life,"
Says Dana B–, "But everything is true.
I remember how all of us would laugh
When father taught us Euclid with a stick

Scratching on the earth and how we'd rub away
The lines if someone came. I remember
When the crayfish died even to the day.
The stream turned dark, but no–one said a thing."

ANTHOLOGY

pauline stainer

EPIPHANY EVE

The meths–drinkers
have bared their chests,
taken flame–water
to escape the gravity
of the flesh.

But even they stop singing
when the three migrating swans
fly over –
red–figured on the retina,
energies that do not burn.

The meths–drinkers
have taken out their eyes,
but still hear the wing–beats
of bodies grown so cold
they no longer shine.

The night is pounced with gold;
the birds bear burial–oils
within their breasts;
and for a moment
the meths–drinkers stagger

stunned by the weightless wings,
the grave kings,
the ghostly directing of the blood.

helen kitson

THE LETTERS

You can say this about me at least:
I was a very dutiful daughter.
I stayed because she needed me,
because I had nowhere else to go.
Because I wanted to do the right thing.

I never married. I had a sweetheart,
she hated him from the first.
He put up with cracked cups & dark
disapproval & *he's got his feet*
under my table. Then the war came.

I wrote him long letters. No reply.
I told you so. I know about bed sores
& where to buy bloomers. I cooked her
food the way she liked it: mushy,
with all the taste removed.

I had hobbies like crochet & gardening.
Few friends. I went to church, I was
well liked, I'm a dutiful daughter;
but if she hadn't died, I think
I'd have killed her.

There was no-one but me to clear up
her debris. No-one was there when I
lifted the lid of her old piano
& found it jammed with his letters.
Hundreds of them. In date order.

That's when I cried, & I've never
cried for my mother. I've stopped
doing crochet, I've lost my faith
& more besides. I'm still well liked,
but I can't stop screaming.

david grubb

THE TERRORS AND MR PETER

Old ladies sometimes called out your name,
clinging to your hand and pulling you into their stained despair,
gripping in their nest of Biblical texts and rolling bosoms and
beaded fables.
Tutors who waited for your stumble, your faltering, your latest
failure
as the Latin loomed, the numbers huddled, the grammar destroyed
all sense
of meaning. Terror of the silences when they would not speak,
mother and father
skirmishing with values, signals of sarcasm, bile of accusation,
careful evasions
wrapped in social ritual. The bleeding buffalo hunters in
nightmares, a hoard
of Sioux surrounding you, or the mouth of Long John Silver
mocking, or the eyes
of those you have most betrayed refusing to diminish. Gang in
the park shouting out
your name, letting down your bike tyres, placing stones in the
centre of snowballs,
threatening to beat up your parents and set your life on fire. Rat
in the basement,
emperor of silences, dictator of darkness, waiting to leap at your
throat, hiding
in your Wellington boots, finally found dead in a box of old rope
but his white eye
looking out, his white eye watching you.
Terror of mother dying, flying away in a psalm of stars, other
people taking over,
father blubbing between his sermons, no voice to answer when
you cry out at night.
A sky of falling birds, feathers smothering, in your mouth even,
smell of millions of
disintegrating wings, fans of bone that coil and attempt flight and
collapse.
Soft tones of the tutor who strokes my knees and puts his hand

up my trousers
as he tells me how I can achieve ten out of ten. Pig killed in the yard,
boiling water and his skin coming off but all the time we see it is Mr. Peter.
Summer days, lying in the byre with Mr. Peter, feeding him maizepulp and
scratching his back, waiting for his grunt.
Cut out his grunt, his sleeping, his summer days, his place on earth; rip
it off him, skin him down past his screaming.
At night when Mr. Peter enters our silences
we bring him maizepulp cakes and drawings of the sun. We sing to him the
summer songs. He sits in a bathchair and wears father's scarf.
Then Sam Frost writes down all Mr. Peter's commands in the back of a prayer book.
They exchange a few jokes, knowing looks and things.
Late afternoon sun passes over like an air balloon.
Somebody is falling out and we all run to see where the body lands.
Already father is there and the choir and a funeral is burying a body
with words.
We throw some maizepulp cakes on the coffin.
Place the earth over the terror.
Place the words over the flowers.
Place the flowers over the snow.
Place the sermon over the rain.
It is raining and we can see Mr. Peter beneath his umbrella
In the haul of early mornings my mother carries a bucketof stars
into the churchyard and decides to drown the kittens
when we are busy at school.

r moulson

ROWING GRANDMA

Your pointy hips were the oarlocks
and your hollow tummy seated two.
We said *Row, Grandma, Row,* and you beat
your arms and raised dust from the carpet.
We said *Row* and your nose pointed true
north and our boat shook with the speed.

As you washed at the sink we saw
your back, a clinker on the sand
at Bridlington, all ribs and keel.
And later, much later, before
you died, you became a shell, a hand
held against the light, a lemon peel.

We said *Make waves,* and then you raised
your skirted knees like sails and pushed
with your feet to jiggle us back
and forwards, or, feet apart, rocked
us from side to side till we lurched
to the floor from your slidey frock.

When we came in, you turned the radio
off, the waves that kept you afloat.
Grandpa brought you from a far place
to live with his folk and made you
happy sad because you found them cold.
In photos yours was a smiley face.

We said *Make a storm, Make a big
sea,* and you pushed hard with your legs
and jerked your tummy off the ground
and bounced and nearly made us sick
till you threw us up to your chest
and held us both there, safe and sound.

For two years after Grandpa died
and beached you among strangers and graves
till we grew too heavy for your tummy
and tired you out ride after ride,
we rowed you crying *Make waves make waves*
and then *Make a big sea, Grandma.*

atar hadari

MILK POWDER

She takes her pay in volumes, mostly literature and fields
too limited in interest to attract crowds paying cash–
she stacks the shelves with dictionaries, embroidering the names
of subject headings on lavender scraps of pale linen–
she thought she'd be a doctor once before the baby came
she told him to be careful and they used things but the shame
was to have to dispose of it at ten on some white room's
raised table and the straps smelling of Dettol so she stayed
at home the first year, took a leave of absence from the course
–they said her dissertation would be waiting, she said "Nurse–
how long should baby–bottle water boil for before use?"
She washed his feet in soap of Pears and tickled his white nose.
Her body that distended like a sack of oranges
retracted slowly, she was slack as suet but the pain
receded– he was gone by then, a man with a young girl
– a colleague, actually, a sister from the school's
  long intellectual struggle.
She spoons heaps of gold into the boy's mouth, dripping milk,
she spoons mounds of paste into the mix to put on price tags'
  backs.
She sits in the window watching leaves fly like the birds
used to rise from her body between small, round pebble breasts
and a belly flat as iron rising to a mount so small
she almost could forget it sometimes, fingering the well
between the books in an alcove, the clove smell of opened paste
and paper in a book not seen the printer's palms since 1912–
the nurses in the brochure hold the baby like a glass
before you – she feels birds rise out
her pussy and fill all the sky with black, migrating feathers.

irene hossack sime

PLEASURE PLACES

I have swept the inside of your teeth with my tongue,
felt the rough stubble of your chin and the hardness of your jaw
on my face. I have enclosed you with my body,
taken you in snow, on carpets and on the telephone.
We've rushed headlong on the beach before we were missed;
waited until after midnight when the house was asleep;
arriving from trains; in a car along quiet lanes;
in the master bedroom of the Wimpey Show Home;
cramped in the toilet of BA 012, where I have let you in.
I have urged you on when you have taken it slow,
shown you where you should go, helped you see the
secret places for our pleasure when you didn't know,
how to be less urgent, lose your composure, give me
time, hear me breathe, know when I don't care where
I am, when I'm swimming outside myself using no stroke,
come where no language exists, gone from where we rest.

sally young

SEDUCING THE LEAD SWAN

Class rehearsals are cancelled.
I'll dance the programme alone,
outstep my cast of rivals –
the cygnets must never know.

Reverse the roles completely.
I want one dance that really lets go,
pulls the hamstrings rigid,
allows our training to show.

I want the smell of scorched sweat
to gild your gasp of surprise –
the clamp of webbed feet on my back,
just the start of it.

ian smith

COMPANY

The weather turns the milk sour,
So we line houseplants outside
For the rain to water and creep
Upstairs to the top room
With the windows open for the storm
That comes across the evening and quietens it,
And chases angels from here to the door,
And stops before we sleep.
The roof glistens in the rain that falls
And soaks the company we keep.

pascale petit

MY SON IS BEAUTIFUL AS THE SUN

(after a painting by Gillermo Kuitka)

His room is long and narrow,
brown as menstrual blood.
His bed-linen is purple.

Every morning I strip his bed.
I have painted a map on his mattress,
with legends of thorns, bones and syringes.

Highways are bloodlines
and land becomes skin --
a hundred miles to the inch.

By midday, I have gathered
the houseplants around his bed,
they are the forest he is lost in.

He sees my head above the fronds
as I pace from corner to corner
reading his last letter:

Dear Ma, I am going into the Interior
to find the bird who wears a shield of sunrays.

My Manakin, my Cock-of-the-Rock.
When I cough, his bird-plumes shrivel.

martha kapos

SUN IN THE KITCHEN

Strong light is very close.
Will I ever find the key
to the mounting evidence:

the planets held in place by your
attraction, the hole in the ozone,
the return of spring?

It's these freak storms.
Shining like a lunatic
your smile plays hell

with all astronomy. And the cold
luminous arc, the dazzling ellipse.
Like watching a drop of water

always just about to fall.
It's the door of a safe slowly
swinging closed on a million

dollar room, spectacularly lit,
a black box shut in the ground
hiding its information like a skull.

But look both ways. Flames play
over the backs of your hands.
Even as we sit faces facing,

bushes break apart and it comes
out into the open. Now it openly
conceals its blazing secret

behind a cloud. Round a bend
a brisk traveller vanishes
down a path like a broken thread.

A few words spoken with calm.
And in the weedy lost mood
of the sea I can just make out

a pale green room rising and falling
near the bottom. There are two
small people sitting at a table.

martha kapos

THE FLOOD

Silly even to think closing
the doors would do any good.
So when the water rose
between the tiles, we thought ok
let's put everything up on slightly
higher shelves, slip bricks under
the corners of the cooker, jack
up the legs of the table. It was then
the river grew large, began running
distractedly like a wounded dog
smelling sweetly of rain, rankly
of earth, poured over the threshold,
flooded the floor, tossing leaves,
a tennis ball of fluorescent green,
the muddled ruins of a coat,
lapped and sucked the furniture,
left foam in the closed drawers.
A pool formed in the dented
crown of a hat. The stuffed chairs
became oddly dark. We could hear it
breathing from the second floor,
a sound of dull concussion beating
quietly in an empty cupboard.

We slept close to it like a heart
at night, an eyelid covering an eye.
How did we know it would be day
inside the room and outside,
filling the corners, the sky and all
available space. Nor could we plan
the way the house would melt
and lose its form, ceilings floating
wide-open and apart, walls
sagging window-frames out of square,
nor how still the varied contents of
the house would lie in new

and strange positions looking up,
and ebb–tide pointing out a wreck,
nor afterwards, on the table,
how carefully the sun would pick
a few cups and spoons, mark
new shadows precisely on the cloth,
and speak their meticulous names:
white, silver, blue.

richard smith–bingham

ENCOUNTER

(i.m Fr. Gerrard White)

Out walking,
large hands clasped mine,
and the sun sprayed off slate roofs.

Not fully aware,
I stared into the light,
who it was had approached me,
was speaking,
september was soft and nostalgic,
inquiring after parents and everyone's health,
brimming with small village sounds,
and what was I doing now,
as though I had lived there all my life,
these many years.

Children spilled out of school,
while he blessed me,
and half–rounded forms in check and blue coats,
still keeping my hands,
looped along with their shopping,
until they tingled.

The light was so long that afternoon,
I never heard a word,
and shadows fled down the street,
they all murmured through me just the same,
then trailed off into the chronic fuzz of motor cars
with their iridescent klaxons.

helen tuschling

GRANDFATHER 1875–1972

They never told me he was dying,
they hardly knew that old man in my head.
The infirmary brick, aloof among the slums,
the scream of braids across my head,
my eyes wide with the oranges and plums
I'd left behind, untidy, by the bed.
No word said to Nurse or Daddy until
too late. I was outside, ill, –
going home. They thought I cried
for the oranges. This hall again
where people lie like dolls, the sheet
a belt across their breasts, the pain
of not daring to move, to peel and eat.
Again the clamour of the nurse's starch
admitting me, a visitor, to break
as he had done the proper march
of death. Placid for my sake
she lay there – wondering, I'm sure,
what I wanted of a broken grey-haired doll –
and I was rude to grandma, who'd endure
another twenty years, terrible and tall.
They never told me he was dying.
They hardly knew that old man in my head.

The rosy brick, the playing fields across
my window, my eyes blind
from time to time with loss,
among the rubies of my life I find
Aunts at Christmas by the plundered tree,
the Austin, and the axe bruising the snow,
the dignities of Parlour Tea
and the pipe-glow outside, to and fro.
The peach brandy he did drink and my eyes
followed her eyes that emptied with each drop.
My russet grandad, now nostalgia triss
my edge of feeling on a broken strop.

They never told me he was dying,
they hardly knew that old man in my head
immortal. Just one note replying
to my condolences when she was dead
holds him upon the bar of time. I keep
his fading years. The sheets where I am lying
are drifts of winters, folded deep.
They never told me he was dying.

jonathan cave

FOXES

I knew them where they were, the dog fox close
beside the leat and vixen on the hill.
They called each other, plaintive and morose,
across the river mists that began to fill
the valley bottom and I lay afraid
until I had placed them, foxes mating
in deep mid-winter.
I have often stayed
short of a gate to watch a vixen waiting
for cubs that tumbled on the aftermath,
and they have vanished; vixens in the gorse
have disappeared; and dog foxes on the path,
unconcerned and leisurely on their course
to the spinney, have dropped from sight
abruptly. They evade by day, sedate
and unobtrusive.
But by night
they become themselves, audacious and elate,
and range again those lands they made demesne
before the first invaders came with tools
of flint to hunt and dibble seeds between
their shelters and the soil around the stools
of ancient oaks and ash trees they had burned
to clear the slopes. Behind their wicker walls
defenceless sleepers woke afraid and turned
to fortify each other, marked the calls
as sinister, and listened through their fears
above the heart-beats pounding in their ears.

gerard donovan

MARCHING SEASON IN BELFASI

Down in the Republic we never bothered
with that King-Billy-and-the-Boyne business

but preserved the date a drinking night
in our small border town, fighting each other instead:

it was always the North, the South, innuendos about,
then into the wet wind of midnight,

hold-me-back shouts outside the pub, each swear
sealed in vapour, each swing drawing blood and politics.

Frank says he understands perfectly
how I might take to killing soon--

how I went religious mad, with collar in one ear,
Prod in the other; half a Provo, half a hand-wringer

between condemnations from cardinals,
cut faces and rosaries. As if nations could be counted on.

It's marching season in Belfast. History lesson:
In Sixteen-Something King Billy bounced Jimmy's men

all the way back to wherever they came from. Ireland
again irredeemably Protestant. Talks about talks about

talks about bloody time for the present tense,
isn't it, says Frank. Frank says I'm stuck,

I'm bored and one year further into a history
that will not remember me. Says get off the fence.

I grew up lonely between a devil and a god,
red hand of Ulster and the southern cross,

deaf from tin whistles, the bang of marching drums:
but I'll breathe heroes into those passions.

I know this gun, I've warmed it in my hand,
broke a man to his knees in a dream or two.

After school I used to watch Frank and his friends
squeeze rounds at the Brits a field and a country away.

They got a soldier one evening in Armagh,
light low in the trees, a shower just passed;

Frank straddles the road on his belly,
aims through the crosshairs' crucifix.

He tells us to hush, he's got the steady hand;
the Brit is guarding a crossroads. Goes down hard.

We'd seen him before. His girlfriend
worked in a coffee shop. She served me

tea and a scone, wore an apron
tied about her neck. I was shy of her.

gary gieddes

DANGLING PARTICIPLE

All afternoon I spent teaching the little snits
participles. Rhymes with nipples.
Yesterday was gerunds. Care less? I doubt

they remember the basic definitions.
Hormones. Scratched on the blackboard:
"The John enters, the whore moans"

Another day: "SIN TAX." Progress,
the Department Head grinned,
wanting me, his wife and three kids

outside in the stationwagon. *Headway,*
giving head. Even with her British accent,
the new Anglican minister offends me

with incorrect usage: *enervate,*
when she obviously means energize,
and "should have went." Queen's

English, right. She should have went
to Grammar School, not seminary. Moral?
Never underestimate the colonies.

3:00 a.m. Gridwork shadows. Drugstore
neon filters through my rattled
blinds. Sounds of aluminium rigging

when he took me at the yacht club.
Frigging, etcetera. Shorthand, vowels
not the only things swallowed

in the heart's vernacular. I woke
from a tryst, speaking tongues, pure
gibberish, ecstatic, soaked,

unfinished, thinking: Why
should I feel guilty, this is *my* dream,
I'll fuck whomever I want.

roger dunn

THE GENDER OF WORDS

A woman's words include – *diaphanous;*
Unfurled, vivacious, limpid, serenade.
Nativity, beseech, sheer, glamorous;
Foundation, quintessential, lemonade.
Forget–me–not, resist, vermilion;
Umbrella, fathomless, cantabile.
Rose, daffodil, narcissus, campion;
Wild orchid, lipstick, perfume, wedding day.
Stilettos, ribbons, "maybe", shed a tear;
Eye–contact, nightingale, bewildered, cry.
Flamenco, Philadelphia, Richard Gere;
Virility, clean–shaven, gallant, shy.
Embraceable, strong, body–language, "No."
Disarmed .. capitulation ... afterglow.

A man's include – *stand fast, enforce, physique;*
Akimbo, Okinawa, pendulum.
Staccato, joie de vivre, lucky streak;
Clandestine, mutineer, delirium.
Majestic, Harlem, rage, impregnable;
Voracious, buccaneer, Catch 22.
Defiant, proposition, tangible;
Submission, overwhelm, revenge, askew.
Voluptuous, cry havoc, renegade;
Glint, ardour, nemesis, reverberate.
Clench, wanderlust, sombrero, fusillade;
Unfettered, nebulous, extrapolate.
Allured, bewitched, curvaceous, breathless, woo;
Seduce .. surrender ... consummate .... "adieu".

k r gladdish

ELIZABETH REFLECTS....

Leicester danced the pinkum–pankum.
Essex brought me verse and silk,
Raleigh sent me furs and parrots,
Burghley fed me lawyer's milk.

Served by all, but still a virgin,
Holy Mary I eclipse.
She of course hatched an immortal,
I've launched only fighting–ships.

I grew up in isolation,
Scared of Kings and Queens and Jacks.
Doomed to a mispronunciation,
On my lips 'sex' came out 'axe'.

frank fell

THROUGH THE BLUE DOOR

I was looking for the country that calls itself blue.
I only wanted to feel at home somewhere,
in the cold hour of just–before–dawn when flowers shrivel,
veils are drawn on the heart's longing, clouds across
the horizon and the sea re–invents its accent,
softening its vowels in the mouth of a river.
It was not only tricks of speech that had me lost,

the clog of modal verbs that tap and dance
like a blind man with a stick – the *musts,*
shoulds, can, couldn'ts that pencilled my map.
It was knowing how far from you I would go:
moonlight dispensing the blue distance,
the lazy hills bent to their future, the sedatives
of forgetting deceptive, and light as river–mist.

August. I've hung around this port for weeks, unable
to unhinge myself and step through the blue door
into days more fragile than eggs. Now it is late,
and already the last ferry gone. Its silent wake
a wishbone pulled and broken, a white tent
pitched on water, striking cerulean currents.
So that, tonight, once more, I will camp beneath

the bluest quilt of hydrangeas, my head pillowed
on a map of leaves, on veins that know the road.
A map my hands fold and unfold with such rhythms
I listen for the lilt of accordions, the sigh
of sea shanties, their waves of colour dissolving
in my skin, blue as a swallower of poison.
Older than the hills, bearded in cobalt and quartz,

I look across time's border breathing its smokey dust,
Its sickly–sweet perfume drifting like a car's exhaust

meg peacocke

VISITANT

That pigjawed god with his thick phallus
who strolled into the garden, glimming
about with snailshell eyes,
crowdark among a sprawl of stems (how
could I swear that I saw him?) snatching
at nerine lilies and cardoon heads
and dragging boughs of half-ripe Bramleys down:
gone, when I turned my head.

But she, pleading some task, has risen
abruptly to go in. That shudder;
that red weal on her neck . . .
How the season is changing! we'll say,
drawing the curtains, loath to remark
on the plum tress, barked and scored, bleeding
new resin, or how something has plundered
the bees' nest in the wall.

brian docherty

A SENSE OF PLACE

This place reminds me of a postcard I saw once,
some industrial town in Germany built in the 50s
by an architect trained in the 30s who thought
Monumental Modernism should last forever.
All very neat & flat with near empty roads and
long glass & ferro–concrete blocks which could be
flats, factories, offices, possibly all 3 in 1.
Dusk is falling, the sodium lights are flaring,
soon it will rain lightly & dark vans will
appear to patrol the area every 20 minutes.
I am not sure how I know this but I do,
I have been in places like this many times,
I think I always get these jobs, not the ones
with exotic beaches, casinos, trans–continental
trains, megalomaniacs & beautiful deadly women.
Being dressed all in black with a knapsack
full of custom–built tools with no makers name,
a machine–pistol & a surprisingly large knife,
is obviously all part of my job description,
so I shall stand under these dark familiar trees
while the fence sizzles like a short–wave radio.
I am not cold, hungry, or thirsty so either
I have not been here long, or long enough
for these needs to have been taken care of.
My pockets hold keys, local money, some cards.
I know it is local money but not which locality
and I cannot read the language in the I.D. cards.
Have I done what I was sent here for?
If the local police tell me where I am,
will I remember who I am? Can I tell them?

james turner

BETWEEN OURSELVES

Our mother is a man who thinks he knows –
his birth certificate says Solihull –
but we remember being embryos
waiting in the womb inside his skull,

re–live our birth (oh, how he loved us then!),
recall our insect–crawl across a page
under the rolling ball–point of his pen.
He brought us up. But now we've come of age

we're not quite what he meant. He's left us free
to mean just what we want to mean. You know,
to him his heart's a riddle. We think he
should look us up again and read us through.
He wouldn't find the answer. Even so,
between ourselves we might provide a clue.

k g chandler

HOMES

"Make yourself at home" they always said
"Give it two flushes" *"Call us Uncle, Aunt"*
(I knew it wasn't like I knew they weren't)
"This is your room". Hospital–cornered bed:

afraid to dent its lines of candlewick...
Should I wait? Or go downstairs? Bowl of fruit
flawless as cellophane, – was it to eat
or, like the loaded bushes, *"just to look"?*

Embroidered cottage text – "HE CARES"; jug
of Honesty lorgnettes; thoughtfully
provided toys almost as good as new;
drawer that opened boy–sized like a morgue...

And when their cheerfulness had run away
(Was it the discovery of a week–old crop
of pee stains dried out like a contour map
under the bed clothes? Or was it how

I *"touched"* things, – that china dog they said
was *"irreplaceable"?* Or failed to be
their long lost son, a furry–necked B.A.
perched like a vulture on the piano lid?)

I couldn't wait to get back to a proper Home:
scuffed lino; smells of overcooking; walls
glossed grey or pink; doorstep butties; bells
that told you where to go; lazy teachers; dorm

of heavy breathers; lav ends; tin bowls; friend
whose insults like a casually flicked towel
at the privates proved less of a betrayal
than those who promised, briefly, to be kind.

andy brown

IN THIS HOUSE, ON THIS MORNING

A plane will glide more easily if rubbed with a candle --
remember to relight the pilot. Light bulbs
last longer & give off more light if you strain them
through old stockings. Use nylons to store opinions.
During a power cut the same rules apply: electricity & water
make a recipe -- use it as a jigsaw puzzle.

An electric lightbulb makes a good mushroom.
Bread can be used to remove light stains.
Dab luminous paint on light switches. Remember
if the head is allowed to dry out completely
when not in use it will crack & break up --
take it off and unplug the holes with a darning needle.

When hanging a long day nap in the right direction,
run a bar of soap along the wrong side & monitor its progress
as you pull it through. Try not to interrupt your work
if you're painting ceilings, walls or floors
as this will tend to make them perish. Use a whisk
to save time. Save time by keeping near the phone.

As your children grow older they are easier to let down.
Prevent this by putting a ball of cotton wool in the end of each
finger.

Write letters & seal them with a little egg white.
Always iron the paper & avoid going in a straight line.
Stagger the line while greasing spots on separate sheets.
Wipe the line clean & free of water droplets.

Put a piece of white paper under each foot. Smooth
some French chalk or talcum over the area before you start
then rub a little paraffin inside your shoes to smarten up
a limp lettuce. If all else fails scour a blocked drain
in this manner: make an X incision in the stem
& check for cracks in folding leaves. Float in the cistern.

Fold in air bubbles for a fluffier poem. Restore a dented
ping pong ball. To make an inconspicuous join
sew decorative patches over worn out places & feelings --
it is easier with an odd number than an even.
International symbols in pattern books make excellent
wastepaper baskets; chilli sauce an unusual cat repellent.

Use manners as a small vice. Slip your hands into plastic
sandwich bags. If you can't change the water every day
use a pastry brush to remove fluff from working parts. If
you can,
use eyebrow tweezers to pull out stray pieces -- you will find it
easier to extract what you want. Put the stone back
into the avocado & seal. & lastly, the skirting.

*The title of the poem is the title of a composition by Wynton Marsalis. It signifies the start of a service in a Baptist church in the Southern black United States.

tim stone

STILL BIRTH

It's never mentioned.
We do not speak of it.
All evidence of it has been erased.
The cot, the kiddies' clothes, the soft toys, have all been sold.
I've even changed the front bedroom back to how it was
Before we put all that Snoopy wallpaper up.

I've returned the baby's blankets we borrowed.
The push-chair has gone back.
I've buried myself in work.
I've tried to forget.
I've tried not to blame myself,
But I can't help wondering if things would be different
If I'd got you to the hospital quicker than I did.

All talk of babies and children is banned from the house.
They are something we thought of, but can no longer have.
We maintain a dignified silence.
We avoid the subject, steer well clear of it,
But the past still conspires to come between us.

You never gave birth to anything living,
But the miscarriage has still left an emptiness
That cannot be filled,
As if something had lived,
When in fact it didn't.

I try to comfort you with a kiss,
But you just turn your head.
I sense you resent even my touch.
I didn't wish to put you through this.
But it couldn't be helped.
I wish I could make things better, but alas I cannot.

I suggested we adopt, but you wouldn't hear of it.
It wouldn't be the same, if it's not your own flesh and blood.

I see your point, but what other choices do we have?
You have given up and lost all hope.
You say you're now incomplete and it can't be put right.
I accept that.
It's bad enough that we can't have a kid,
But what's worse is they had to cut bits out of you like they did.

jamie lawson

FISH

Some of the fish turned to gold,
these were called goldfish.
All of the veins in the body lead to the same place,
this was called the heart.
As a present, on your birthday,
I gave you a rich fish.
In return you gave me your last breath.

william morley

SPOONS

I feel the gentle press,
The pleasant squidge
Of her breast on my back;
The round neat curve of your shoulder
Sunk on mine in a Klimt Kiss;
I hear the rustle of her legs
On the sheets
Moving to tuck under mine
Foetally;
The hairs of the tops of your thighs
Brush, nestle and rest intertwined
With those of mine -
Encircling, encircled,
Fatefully;
Her soft belly traps warmth - a pocket
In the small of my back,
In her dark, dark navel.

From there
I feel the energy of the corridor of the future;
I'm at a point where I belong:
An umbilical cord of energy so long
It includes me
And stretches on and on
Into infinity

I hear the silent 'ka'
Of lips parting, sucking in air
At my ear
And the gentle sigh as she exhales,
I sense the tiny click
Of a pursed-lip smile
And anticipate the moment
Before you move lightly to lean over
And kiss the pixie-tip of my ear:
Click, again. Click -

Your smile settles quietly back on her pillow
Behind,
Watchful,
Knowing I know.

ann gilchrist

INCANTATION

Astride my besom,
Flaying, black velvet cape,
Purple Janet Reger silk knickers,
matching talons
Enveloped in Obsession
by Calvin Klein,
I scour the night,
Plotting to hex,
those who have crossed me,
with compulsory readings
from 'Hello' Magazine,

I make acid green images
from Play–Doh,
stick in pins,
delivering retribution
to the person who scratched
my broomstick
parking on Sainsburys.

Send my Familiar
to the house of my husband's mistress,
who becomes fat, wrinkly,
gets dogs breath.

Drift on thermals,
winds, not Damart,
into the arms of
Merlin, the warlock,
dark, and skilled
in Orphic erotica.

Carmine streaks across the sky
signal the end of night flights.

I used to be a social worker.

joan sampson tucker

THERMALS

We all admire your sunburnt profile,
grotesque, inhuman though it is:
chisel–featured, hollow–eyed;
there, snarling into isobars
you salivate through mossy gums
for beetles, snakes and bats.

Mass belies your powerlessness
to ban those sweeps of chalk and paint
describing lines and circles in your gorge;
likewise the constant scratch and tickle
we impose with climbing tackle
to get–even with your height.

And so we creep around your ears
to inch along a cheek–bone ridge,
grab an eyebrow, squat in turn
astride your nose–bridge, rest ...
before attempting to surmount
your temples – higher still.

Struggling through your widow's peak
we fight out way through wind–swept scrub
and force a parting towards your crown
whose smooth rock baldness proves to be
a resting place just right for sprawlers
gulping gusts of mountain air.

When rising heatwaves scorch the skinks
we slither downward, swinging out
to kick against your mindless head
until at base, we dump our gear
and race to slurp the icy water
from the runnels of your face.

Its stinging splash reminds us now
that human blood is warm – so different
from that chilly stuff pulsating through
'the veins of frogs whose nature is
content to leap mere pebble–height
in the sparkle of your tears.

john latham

THE SOUND OF O

My bed high, cold. Striped pillow tastes of vinegar,
my new pyjamas have no memories.

Why did she serve me strawberries
in our willow-pattern bowl
the day the ambulance took me away?
It was their sweat gave me scarlet fever.

Each afternoon they take me to a tall, thin room,
I see her face, green felt hat
at the far end of a tunnel sealed by glass
that swallows my plea to take me home, my promise
not to write wicked words on the window-sill again

that twists her mouthing, unfocuses her eyes.
I'm waving back, but she can't see me.

The boy in the next bed has a cage over his legs.
Nurse whispers they're withered
with a wasting disease.
I dream them thin and dry under his sheet
until they snap like bracken.
When I ask him if he'll die
he says "I punish liars to doom",
won't look at me again
not even as they trolley him away.

Ten weeks. I no longer ache to touch her,
inhale her washday scent of suds and starch,
I ask Nurse Cora for bedtime stories now.

Not the violence of the wind
but the sound it makes, the o,
the o of isolation hospital, sorrow, polio,
the o her mouth made
when I spat at her through tempered glass.

ACCOUNTING
for
BEGINNERS

by

JAMES DOVEY

LECTURER IN ACCOUNTING, COMMERCE AND ECONOMIC ORGANISATION, CROYDON COLLEGE 1967–1980

A textbook for pre-study and to provide simplification, clarification and illustration of common difficulties experienced during early studies; of value to students, teachers, small businesses, the self employed and those concerned with Business Computing

Whilst every care has been taken to ensure the accuracy of the addresses and telephone numbers contained in the appendixes in this book at the time of going to press, such information is subject to change.

Printed in Great Britain at the University Press, Cambridge

173 Chaldon Way
Coulsdon Surrey CR5 1DP
ISBN 0 9517472 1 5

First published 1991
New edition 1992

CONTENTS

PREFACE

The moment when a student grasps a concept which is difficult is one of the best things about learning and teaching. It means that a way through has been found which makes sense.

For many years of teaching the author has conducted research to ascertain what is needed by beginners to understand the logic of debits and credits within the basic structure of accounts, to see the reasons for the way in which they are applied to transactions and to appreciate the common sense of the meanings given to them. His conclusions, which have been tested on many students, are the basis for the text of Accounting for Beginners.

A large number of students find textbooks designed for use in the classroom difficult to cope with when no teacher is at hand to act as interpreter. Even when they are able to learn from them the practice, they find it difficult to understand the theory.

Many different attempts in many different ways have been made to explain debits and credits. Most beginners start their studies with a view of debit and credit which is the opposite of the view taken in the structure of accounts. The author believes that the only satisfactory way of making the application of debits and credits to accounting clear and logical, is by illustrating how they are used as plus and minus within the mathematical structure, to satisfy the formula which produces the profit or loss and the assets and liabilities.

Adherence in the UK to the traditional double sided form of Balance Sheet has resulted in complexities in the early stages of studies. It shows the TOTAL gross assets as equal to the TOTAL of the owner's interest AND the liabilities to the outside world. Although the latter two items are both means of financing the assets which is useful information, their total is not one side of the accounting equation on which the mathematical structure of the accounts is based. Right at the start of his studies the beginner should understand that the central and main purpose of the structure of accounts is to equate the owner's interest, the amount invested or the capital liability with the net worth of the business. When the vertical form of Balance Sheet is understood at the outset, together with the true equation and the mathematical formula which produces it, many subsidiary matters are simplified.

The text, illustrations and exercises, have been tested in teaching situations and submitted to professionals, including the Director of Technical Services of the Institute of Cost and Management Accountants.

Whatever course of studies any student undertakes which includes Bookkeeping or Accounting, an understanding of the contents of 'Accounting for Beginners' will be invaluable in assimilating the instruction received in the classroom, whatever form this may take and whatever main textbook he is called upon to use. Also, an appreciation of the evaluation of debits and credits as plus and minus in the mathematical structure of accounts will be of great assistance as this leads naturally to computerisation.

For those running a small business, or self-employed, sufficient instruction is provided for understanding the basic structure of accounts and their value in providing information for sound management, monetary control and the information required for producing a Profit and Loss Account and a Balance Sheet.

In addition to its function in supplementing classroom studies for students of 18 years of age upwards, the text has been designed to be intelligible to pupils as young as 11 in 11–16 secondary schools – certainly at 14 – as well as to students in the 16–18 group intending to go on to further and higher education.

It is also suitable for a short course of instruction where Bookkeeping or Accounting is included in Liberal Studies in technical colleges, in their departments of engineering, building, food trades, etc.

The explanations and instructions contained in the text and illustrations give those who handle computers a better understanding of input and output of accounting data. This is of considerable value to staff of professional accountants and to students undertaking studies involving the computerisation of accounts.

One of the aims of the book is to create a sound foundation of understanding of the mathematical structure of accounts, in students undertaking courses set by bodies such as the GCSE Examining Boards, The Business and Technician Education Council (BTEC), The London Chamber of Commerce and Industry (LCCI), The RSA Examinations Board, The City and Guilds of London Institute, The Chartered Institute of Bankers (CIB), The Chartered Insurance Institute (CII), The Institute of Chartered Secretaries and Administrators (ICSA), The Chartered Institute of Management Accountants (CIMA), The Chartered Association of Certified Accountants (CACA), The Association of Accounting Technicians (AAT) or The Institute of Financial Accountants (IFA).

TO THE STUDENT

Treat the questions at the end of each chapter as if they were on an examination paper. Do not look at the answers given in the book until you have completed your own. This will enable you to see and learn from your mistakes and identify necessary revision.

Be aware that whatever modern methods are used to produce accounts they must be controlled by the same concepts, principles and basic mathematical structure as those which govern the manual system. This is a proper foundation for all further business studies and essential for small businesses unable to afford expensive equipment.

Whether you are self-employed, running a business, looking for promotion, or seeking to increase your fitness for a job, a knowledge of accounting is invaluable.

If you intend to study for a career in Banking, Insurance, Administration, Finance, Business Management or Business Computing, this book will give you a head start and stand you in good stead throughout whatever course you undertake. A list of useful addresses, telephone numbers and contacts are provided in the Appendix.

INTRODUCTION

Accounting uses mathematics and language in special forms suited to it. It arranges figures for adding and subtracting in a special way which is called ACCOUNT FORM and gives to many words special meanings which are different to their meanings in ordinary speech.

For example, in accounting a DEBIT is plus (+), meaning an increase in business wealth or the receipt of value, and a CREDIT is minus (−), meaning a decrease in business wealth or the giving of value. VALUE is money or anything exchanged for money.

Note that the word 'debit' has an entirely different meaning to the word 'debt'. A debit describes any item which is treated as plus (+) whereas a debt may be either debit (+) or credit (−) according to whether it is money owed to a business or by a business.

The word 'DEBIT' is also used to describe a charge. The word 'CREDIT' is also used to describe an allowance. A charge or debit is plus (+) for the one who gives it, but it is minus (−) for the one to whom it is given. An allowance or a credit is minus (−) for the one who gives it, but it is plus (+) for the one to whom it is given.

If one is charged or receives a bill or a debit, one is less well off and must calculate the decrease in one's own wealth with a credit (−). If one makes a charge or gives a bill or a debit to someone else, one is better off and must calculate the increase in one's wealth with a debit (+). If one receives an allowance or a credit, one is better off and must calculate the increase in one's own wealth with a debit (+). If one makes an allowance or gives a credit to someone else, one is less well off and must calculate the decrease in one's own wealth with a credit (−).

A TRANSACTION is an exchange of value and is treated as both debit (+) and credit (−) because value is both received and given in exchange.

To RECORD a transaction is to put it in writing or keep evidence of it in some other suitable way. This usually requires entries in accounts.

An ENTRY in the books is an entry in an account consisting of a note of the date of a transaction and its value in terms of money.

A BALANCE is the result of adding or taking away, that is addition and subtraction, in pounds and pence.

The ASSETS of a business are its possessions – the things of value which it holds or has in its possession.

The LIABILITIES of a business are the debts which it owes.

At the beginning of the study of accounting it is important that the following ACCOUNTING CONCEPTS be noted, and that they be borne in mind throughout the whole study. Accounting concepts are ideas, recipes or formulas which act as guides to the practice of accounting. They contain principles or rules which must be followed.

THE BUSINESS ENTITY CONCEPT. The accounts of a business record only those transactions which concern or affect that part of the wealth of the owner or proprietor of the business which has been separated from his total personal or private wealth and put into the business as the invested capital of the business. *For accounting purposes a business is considered to be an entity or thing which is separate and distinct from its owner, to whom it is accountable or responsible.*

As an example, suppose that a certain Mr A. Bell has personal money and belongings totalling £25,000 and invests £19,000 of this in a business. The business is not concerned with what happens to the £6,000 which Mr Bell has kept in his own possession. The business is, however, very much concerned with and responsible to Mr Bell for what happens to the £19,000 which he has invested or laid out in the business. The business must, therefore, record every transaction or piece of business which it puts through so that it can show Mr Bell whether his investment has increased by the making of a profit or decreased by the making of a loss. It must also show whether it is able to meet its liabilities, that is to say pay its debts.

For accounting purposes 'THE BUSINESS' can be considered as a vessel or container of no value in itself, holding or having in its possession things of real value which belong to its owner.

In recording its possessions the business must always show itself as OWNING none, because its possessions belong to its owner. For this purpose every statement of the value in its possession must be counterbalanced by another statement of the debt it owes, in respect of that value, to its proprietor. Possessions referred to as owned by a business, whether they are held in possession of the business or in the hands of some third party in the outside world, are in fact owned by the proprietor of the business.

To do this in the accounts, a business records its possessions as positive (+), and records the counterbalancing debt to the real owner of the possessions as negative (−). As both records are of equal monetary value or amount, they cancel each other out.

	£
Value in possession of Mr. Bell's business at start	19,000 (+)
Debt owing to Mr. Bell at start	19,000 (-)

Mathematically, the entries in the accounts balance out or result in an answer of NIL (0). Alternatively, one can say that the total value held by the business, as shown in the accounts, is equal in amount to the amount of the debt owed by the business to its owner, as also shown in the accounts.

	£
Total assets	19,000
Liability to owner	19,000

It should be understood that although the Business Entity Concept is only concerned with two entities – the business and its owner – there are other entities to be recognised in studying the activities and organisation of a business. There is a third entity in the form of the bank which is appointed to look after whatever money the business possesses but has not yet used, and a fourth entity in the form of the world outside the business and apart from its owner and its banker.

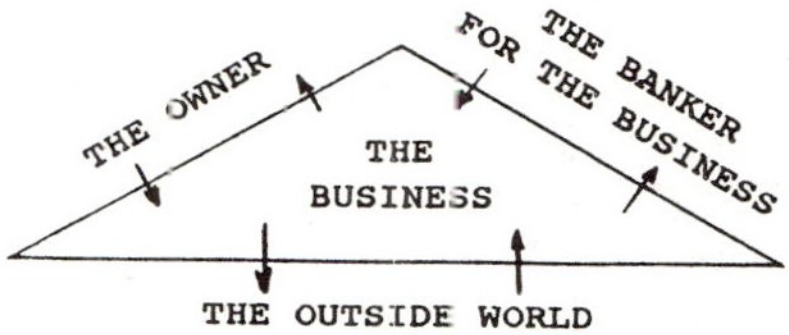

Money flows between the business and its proprietor. Money flows between the business and its bank. Money and value in a variety of other forms flow between the business and the outside world.

THE DUALITY CONCEPT. A journey made by a traveller can be recorded from two points of view. The journey is made up of both a departure and an arrival. The starting place has parted with the traveller and, therefore, has one traveller less, which it could record with a minus (−). The place of destination has one traveller more, which it could record with a plus (+). The two opposite results of the journey make up its duality.

A transaction has a dual result for both persons concerned. For instance, when a packet of tea is bought or purchased from a shopkeeper, the buyer parts with money (minus) and the seller receives money (plus). At the same time the buyer receives tea (plus) and the seller parts with tea (minus). The duality for the buyer is the giving of money and the receipt of tea. The duality for the seller is the receipt of money and the giving of tea.

Every business transaction results in a movement of value so that the same value in monetary terms is both given and received by both of those concerned – both parties to the transaction. Each of the parties both gives one kind of value and receives another kind of value in exchange.

As a business must record the amount in money of every kind of value which it has in its possession, it must record, for every transaction, the monetary value of what it receives and the monetary value of what it parts with in exchange. This concept of duality, together with the Business Entity Concept, form the basis or foundation on which the mathematics of accounting are built. *From this basis the DOUBLE ENTRY SYSTEM of bookkeeping has been evolved or developed, which requires a separate entry to be made in each of two different accounts in respect of every transaction, one entry for value received being called a debit* (+) *and the other for value given being called a credit* (−).

In account form all debits (+) are placed on the left and all credits (−) are placed on the right. As an example, the translation of the sum 1 + 3 − 2 = 2 into account form is carried out as follows:

Place the pluses on the left and the minus on the right

+ (debit)	(credit) −
1	2
3	

The minus side requires 2 more to make it equal to the total of the plus side. The result is, therefore, +2. To show this, place '2' in the minus side as a balance or answer carried down, total and rule off both sides which will then be equal, and place the answer '2' underneath, in the plus side:

+ (debit)	(credit) -
1	2
3	c/d 2
4	4
B/d 2	

2+2−6, worked out in account form would appear as –

Debit (+)		Credit (-)	
	2		6
	2		
Balance carried/d	2		
	6		6
		Balance b/down	2

The answer is minus 2 or a credit balance of 2.

Ignoring for the moment details of the way in which accounts are correctly headed and made up, the principles of the Duality Concept explained above are illustrated in account form in the following examples, just to show how an entry on the left side records value received, an entry on the right side records value parted with, and the heading describes the kind of value which has been received or given.

A. Smith buys a 10p packet of tea and pays the seller, B. Brown, 10p for it.

A. Smith could record this transaction as follows:

CASH

Debit (+)	Credit (-)
	10p

TEA

Debit (+)	Credit (-)
10p	

B. Brown could record this transaction as follows:

CASH

Debit (+)	Credit (-)
10p	

TEA

Debit (+)	Credit (-)
	10p

Within the concept of duality, the creation of a debt has the same effect on both parties to a transaction as a movement of money. A debt is created when something is bought or sold, no money changes hands at the time of the transaction, and there is, instead, agreement that payment will be made at some later date. At the time of the transaction, although no money changes hands, the ownership of money does change from one of the parties to the other. Money owed belongs to the party to whom it is owed. Consequently, when a debt is created or established, value is given by the party who owes the money and received by the party to whom the money is owed.

A. Smith buys a 10p packet of tea from B. Brown, takes possession of the tea and promises to pay B. Brown for it at a later date.

A. Smith could record this transaction as follows:

DEBT OWED TO B. BROWN	
Debit (+)	Credit (-)
	10p

TEA	
Debit (+)	Credit (-)
10p	

B. Brown could record this transaction as follows:

DEBT OWED BY A. SMITH	
Debit (+)	Credit (-)
10p	

TEA	
Debit (+)	Credit (-)
	10p

When a debt is paid, another transaction of a dual kind is made – actual money is exchanged for the debt. The debt is cancelled and both parties are back in the same position as they would have been if the actual money had been paid at the time of the first transaction.

A. Smith pays 10*p to B. Brown for the packet of tea which he has previously purchased with a promise to pay later.*

Using the records already established when he purchased the tea, as illustrated in the last example, and adding a new record for the money which has now been paid, A. Smith would record the payment by showing the debt cancelled and the cash parted with:

DEBT OWED TO B. BROWN	
Debit (+)	Credit (-)
10p	10p

TEA	
Debit (+)	Credit (-)
10p	

CASH	
Debit (+)	Credit (-)
	10p

In a similar way, B. Brown would record the payment by showing the debt cancelled and the cash received:

DEBT OWED BY A. SMITH	
Debit (+)	Credit (-)
10p	10p

TEA	
Debit (+)	Credit (-)
	10p

CASH	
Debit (+)	Credit (-)
10p	

Students are sometimes puzzled by the fact that a Bank Statement shows the monies paid into it as credits (−). The reason for this becomes clear if it is understood that when a person or business pays money into a bank, a debt is created. The money is still an asset (debit +) of the bank's customer and is a liability (credit −) of the bank to its customer. In the same way as a business must, as part of a dual or double entry, show its liability to its owner as a credit (−), so the bank, as part of its own dual entry, must show the money it has received from the business as a credit (−). The bank will also have a record of the money it is holding for the business, to complete its own dual entry, but this does not concern its customer, the business.

THE MANAGEMENT CONCEPT. The amount of success which a business has in carrying out whatever it has been formed to do, in fact its very existence, depends upon what its management – the person or persons who run it – decides to do from day to day. As well as knowing what profit or loss has been made by a business, and how able it is to meet its financial commitments – pay its debts – its management requires the greatest possible amount of information which is useful to it in carrying out its task. Whilst a set of accounts must be planned or designed to result in accurate calculations of profit or loss and statements of assets and liabilities, it must also be arranged in such a way as to give management as much as possible of the facts and figures which it needs to run the business well. It is not enough, for instance, to tell management how much profit or loss has been made. Management requires to know the total amounts of each of the different kinds of costs and expenses, and the amount of money obtained from what has been sold, which have caused a profit or loss to be made. It needs to know how much money the business has at its bank and on its premises, and how much money is owed to the business and by the business. It wants to see the differences between what has happened in one period of time and what has happened in another period of time. It requires much other information, as will be seen as the study of business accounting advances.

It should also be understood that the quickly changing state of affairs of a business requires that management information always be up to date and quickly available, otherwise it may be too late to be of much use.

There are other accounting concepts, and accepted practices called accounting conventions, which will be explained in suitable places later in the book. Another preliminary aid to the use of accounts, and the mathematics used in them, is a clear understanding of the following simple rules.

PLUS means more than nil, zero or naught (0), or an addition.

MINUS means less than nil, or a subtraction.

'c/d' means 'carried down'. 'b/d' means 'brought down'.

'c/f' means 'carried forward'. 'b/f' means 'brought forward'.

The calculations illustrating the following rules are shown in three forms. Firstly in horizontal form, secondly in vertical, tabular, or columnar form, and thirdly in account form.

To INCREASE a PLUS one must use a PLUS:

1 + 1 = 2

1 +
1 +
——
2 +
══

Debit		Credit	
	1	Balance c/d	2
	1		
	2		2
Balance b/d	2		

To DECREASE a PLUS one must use a MINUS:

2 - 1 = 1

2 +
1 -
——
1 +
══

Debit		Credit	
	2		1
		Balance c/d	1
	2		2
Balance b/d	1		

1 - 2 = -1

1 +
2 -
——
1 -

Debit		Credit	
	1		2
Balance c/d	1		
	2		2
		Balance b/d	1

To INCREASE a MINUS one must use a MINUS:

-1 - 1 = -2

1 -
1 -
——
2 -

Debit		Credit	
Balance c/d	2		1
			1
	2		2
		Balance b/d	2

To DECREASE a MINUS one must use a PLUS:

-2 + 1 = -1

2 -
1 +
——
1 -

Debit		Credit	
	1		2
Balance c/d	1		
	2		2
		Balance b/d	1

-1 + 2 = 1

1 -
2 +
——
1 +

Debit		Credit	
	2		1
		Balance c/d	1
	2		2
Balance b/d	1		

The terms 'GROSS' and 'NET' should be clearly understood. The gross weight of a case of goods is the total of the weight of the goods and the weight of the case. The net weight of the case of goods is the weight of the goods alone, that is the total weight less the weight of the case. In the same way, if an article which cost 9p is put into a box which cost 1p, the total cost of the article and the box is the gross cost (10p). The cost of the article alone is the net cost (10p − 1p = 9p). The gross assets of a business is the total amount of all its assets BEFORE deduction therefrom of the total of all its liabilities to the outside world. This is called TOTAL ASSETS, or simply THE ASSETS. The net assets of a business is the total amount of all its assets remaining AFTER deduction therefrom of the total of its liabilities to the outside world. This is called TOTAL NET ASSETS or NET WORTH.

If the amount of one's possessions, or assets is greater than the amount of one's debts, or liabilities, one has a plus (+) amount, or SURPLUS, of wealth, net worth or total NET assets:

£
2 (+) possessions
1 (-) debts
——
1 (+) net worth

Assets	£	Liabilities	£
	2		1
		Net worth c/d	1
	2		2
Net worth b/d	1		

The NET WORTH or TOTAL NET ASSETS of a business is calculated by deducting its debts TO THE OUTSIDE WORLD from the total of the assets which it holds. This net worth is counterbalanced by the liability of the business to its owner, as previously explained:

	£
Total assets	2 (+)
Liabilities (to outside world)	1 (-)
Total NET assets	1 (+)
Capital (liability to owner)	1 (-)

If one's debts amount to more than the amount of one's possessions, one has a minus (−) amount, or DEFICIENCY, of wealth, net worth or total NET assets:

£
1 (+) possessions
2 (-) debts
——
1 (-) net worth

Assets	£	Liabilities	£
	1		2
Deficiency c/d	1		
	2		2
		Deficiency b/d	1

How such a state of affairs in a business is related to its owner and the capital he has invested in it is left to later studies.

The debit (+) side of an account can also be thought of as the debtor side. The credit (−) side of an account can also be thought of as the creditor side. This has led to the recognised abbreviations for debtor or debit and for creditor or credit which are 'Dr' and 'Cr'. Money owed to a business is owed by a 'debtor' of the business. Money owed by a business is owed to a 'creditor' of the business.

The student should practice carefulness, write clearly, and make good figures which can be read without any possibility of being misunderstood. He should also be determined enough to find out the meaning of words which are new to him but not explained in the book, by using a dictionary or by asking questions.

As each new piece of knowledge is obtained it makes what has gone before easier to understand. For this reason, the whole of each chapter should be read right through to firstly see an overall picture of its contents, and then studied paragraph by paragraph to obtain complete understanding of all the information and instruction which it contains.

MATHEMATICAL FORMULA FOR THE DOUBLE ENTRY SYSTEM OF ACCOUNTING

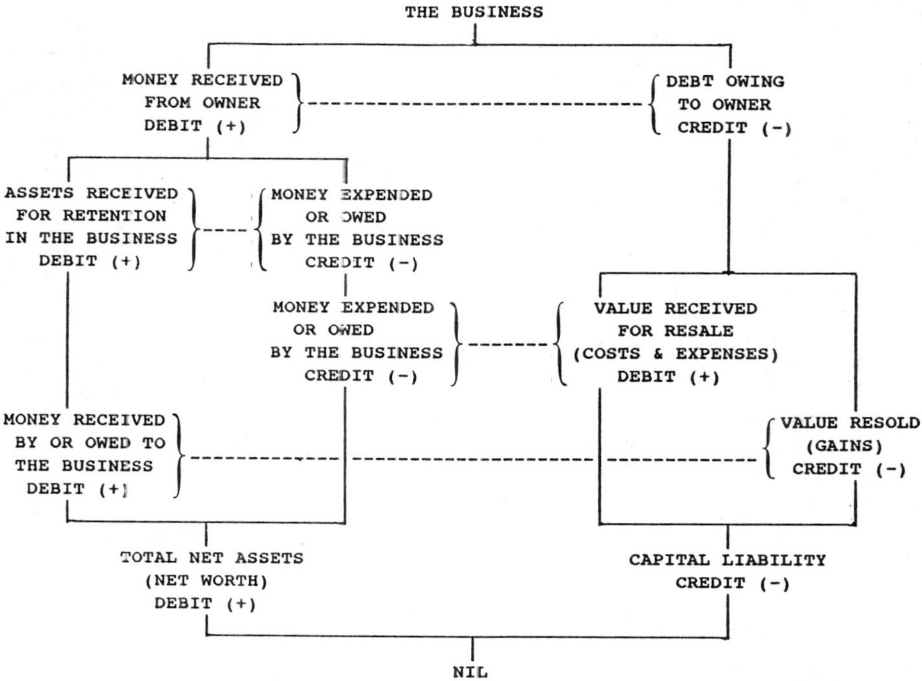

The two parts of each pair of entries, shown horizontally opposite each other, are equal in monetary value or amount. Each pair represents a type of transaction.

The first pair represents an investment in a business.

The second pair represents an exchange of one kind of asset for a different kind of asset, neither of which are intended for resale. This kind of transaction makes no difference to the amount of the Total Net Assets, nor to the amount of the Capital Liability. It does, however, create a change in the composition or make-up of the Total Net Assets.

The third pair represents the exchange of money for goods and services to be resold. It decreases the amounts of both the Total Net Assets with a credit (−) and the Capital Liability with a debit (+).

The fourth pair represents the re-exchange of the goods and services for money. It increases the amounts of both the Total Net Assets with a debit (+) and the Capital Liability with a credit (−).

If the amount of money given or owed by the business in exchange for value received for resale is less than the amount of money received or owed to the business as a result of the resale of that value, a profit is made and both total net assets and capital liability are equally increased.

The formula is shown as a guide to future studies. It is later repeated with sums of money inserted to illustrate the calculations which it controls. Later still, it is shown again as a framework or accounts containing the basic double entries and final moves which it dictates.

It will be seen that the formula channels the pluses (debits) and the minuses (credits) in the accounts in two directions; one, as shown on the left of the diagram, into the calculation of the Total Net Assets or Net Worth of a business, and the other, as depicted on the right of the diagram, into the calculation of the Capital Liability of the business to its owner. No matter what the actual figures may be, provided that each pair of figures consists of a debit (+) and a credit (−) of the same amount, the net result of all the debits (+) and credits (−) used to calculate the Total Net Assets must be the opposite but equal in amount to the net result of all the debits (+) and credits (−) used to calculate the Capital Liability. This being so, the overall result of putting both calculations together mathematically must be NIL (0).

To ensure a proper understanding of the mathematical structure of accounts, imagine that you started a business, and what the results were at the close of the first year of trading. Confine your chosen figures to the following:

(*a*) The amount you invested (CAPITAL).
(*b*) Total cost of equipping the business for operations (FIXED ASSETS).
(*c*) Total cost of goods purchased and resold, plus the expenses of running the business such as rent, electricity, telephones, stationery, wages paid, etc. (COSTS AND EXPENSES).
(*d*) Total amount received for goods sold (SALES).

EXAMPLE: (a) £30,000 (b) £20,000 (c) £65,000 (d) £60,000

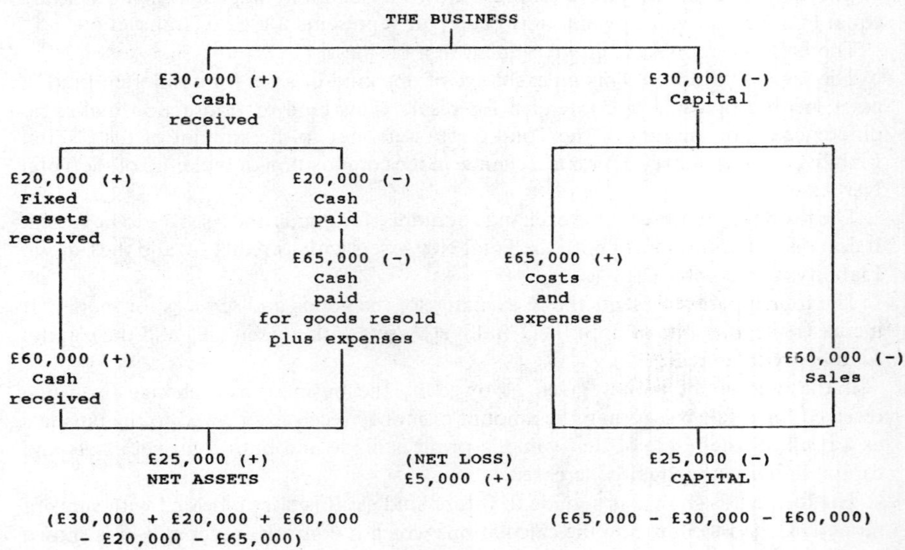

Reproduce the diagram shown above, inserting the figures you have chosen. Calculate, as at the end of the year, your net assets from the left-hand side, your capital liability from the right-hand side, and your profit or loss for the year. Insert these figures at the foot of the diagram to complete it. Remember that both the net assets and the capital liability will have increased by the amount of profit or decreased by the amount of loss, as the case may be.

The plus signs may be replaced by 'Dr' and the minus signs by 'Cr'. The figures used represent totals extracted from a number of individual accounts.

To gain the maximum benefit from this exercise it should be repeated several times, inventing different figures each time.

CHAPTER 1

Debits and Credits

The 'Double Entry' system of bookkeeping is based on the recording of every single transaction entered into by a business, in two opposite but equal forms, one positive (+) called a debit and the other negative (−) called a credit.

Firstly it is necessary to consider the business itself in its two opposite but equal forms: on the one side the business and on the other its proprietor. The one entity is separated into two. Both the business and its proprietor will make, each in their own separate records, two entries in respect of every single transaction entered into between them.

Mr A. Bell decides to commence a business and pays into it out of his private funds £19,000 which becomes the capital of the business as distinct from his private capital. The business must record that it has a liability to its proprietor, Mr Bell and in his private records Mr Bell will record that he has an asset which is his investment in the business. The former will be recorded as a credit (−) in the books of the business and, in, his private records, Mr Bell will record it as debit (+). We shall, however, henceforward be concerned only with the records kept by the business.

So far as the business is concerned it will not only be necessary to record this transaction as a credit (−), but also to record it as a debit (+) to complete the double entry. It must be recorded in its two opposite but equal forms. (Mr Bell will also record it in two forms in his private records but we are not now concerned with this aspect of the transaction.) The two aspects which must be recorded in the books of the business are as follows:

(i) A record of the money possessed which is an ASSET of the business and a DEBIT (−).

(ii) A record of the LIABILITY of the business to its proprietor Mr Bell (in respect of this asset) which is a CREDIT (−).

These records are made in accounts in which the debits are placed on the left side and the credits on the right. Each account is given a name to indicate what it records and each entry records only one side of the two opposite but equal forms of a transaction. Each transaction requires a single entry on opposite sides in each of two different accounts to complete the double entry. The two accounts and entries therein for the above transaction would appear as follows:

Dr (+)			CASH		Cr (-)
Date	Capital A. Bell	£19,000			

Dr (+)			CAPITAL A. BELL		Cr (-)
			Date	Cash	£19,000

In the Cash Account the asset of cash is shown as having been received in respect of capital and in the Capital Account the liability to the proprietor is shown as having been created by the receipt of cash. All double entries are cross referenced in this way. As entries are built up in accounts a history is recorded of the item represented by the heading of each account. This can be seen by reference to the illustrations of accounts in Chapter 6.

The equation used for the Double Entry system of accounting depends upon two different meanings which are attached to the term 'CAPITAL'.

In a positive sense the capital of a business consists of possessions such as:

Property, plant, machinery, furniture, transport vehicles etc.
Money.
Debts receivable which represent money belonging to the business but not actually in its possession. They are described as DEBTORS.
Stocks of goods held for resale.

Such possessions are named ASSETS and recorded in the accounts as debits (+).

In a negative sense the capital of a business is its proprietor's investment in the business. The assets, as described above, belong to the proprietor who, by his investment, has paid for them. The business must record not only the assets which it has in its possession but also the liability it has to its proprietor as a result of his investment in the assets.

This liability to the proprietor is named THE CAPITAL and recorded in the Capital Account as a credit (−).

The first asset possessed by Mr Bell's business was the cash which it received from Mr Bell for his investment, the ASSET of cash being equal to the CAPITAL invested. These facts were recorded in the accounts as already illustrated.

Liabilities other than the capital liability, that is to say debts payable to persons or units other than the proprietor, are described as CREDITORS. They represent that part of the cash possessed which belongs to persons or units other than the proprietor. They reduce the total value of the assets possessed, which include cash, and are recorded as credit (−) entries in accounts for the persons or units to whom they are payable. As the same time the value received by the business as a result of their creation equally INCREASES the total value of the assets possessed. Their creation brings about a change in the composition of the assets but no change in the total net value of the assets.

TOTAL NET ASSETS = CAPITAL

The accounting equation can be expressed as follows:

TOTAL NET ASSETS − CAPITAL LIABILITY = 0

This is illustrated by listing in vertical form and totalling the entries shown in the accounts, as follows:

	£	
Asset of Cash	19,000	(debit +)
Capital Liability	19,000	(credit -)
	NIL	

Profit results from the exchange of money for goods and services, and the re-exchange of the goods and services for a greater amount of money than was parted with in order to acquire them. Thus, in a positive sense, profit is an increase in assets possessed.

In a negative sense profit is also an increase in the proprietor's investment in the business. The whole of the assets belong to the proprietor whatever their total value may be at any time. Therefore, the business must not only record the increase in assets which a profit produces, but also record the corresponding increase which that profit brings about in the capital liability of the business to its proprietor.

An increase in the total value of assets is AUTOMATICALLY brought about in the accounts when a profit is made. If money is exchanged for other kinds of assets no change takes place in the total value of the assets and no profit is made. When, however, assets other than money are sold for more than their cost, less money is paid away when they are acquired than is received when they are sold; consequently, the profit made is automatically included, in its positive sense, in the entries made in the Cash Account in respect of monies paid away and received.

The equivalent increase in the capital liability is arrived at by a separate calculation. In addition to recording in the Cash Account the amount of money received from a sale, the amount of the sale is recorded separately as a GAIN. Also, in addition to recording in the Cash Account the amount of money paid away when the asset sold was acquired, the amount of the acquisition is recorded separately as a COST or EXPENSE. The cost or expense is then set against the gain in order to calculate the amount of profit which must be added to the capital liability.

If, for instance, Mr Bell's business paid away cash for £45,000 worth of goods and services, and received back £50,000 cash for the sale of those goods and services, the entries in the Cash Account would automatically record the positive increase in assets, and the separate calculation of the negative increase in the capital liability would be:

Gain	£50,000 (credit -)
Costs & expenses	45,000 (debit +)
Profit	£ 5,000 (credit -)

The capital invested in a business by its proprietor is, as previously shown, recorded as a liability with a credit (−) entry in the Capital Account:

Dr (+)	CAPITAL	A. BELL	Cr (-)
	Date	Cash	£19,000

Profit made by a business belongs to its proprietor and therefore, if not withdrawn, increases the capital liability of the business to its proprietor. As capital liability is recorded as a credit (−) entry in the Capital Account, the profit made must also be recorded therein as a credit (−) entry, as follows:

Dr (+)	CAPITAL	A. BELL	Cr (-)
	DATE	CASH	£19,000
	"	Profit	5,000
			£24,000

In accounting language a distinction is sometimes made between GAINS and PROFITS. For the sake of clarity, in this book the term GAIN is used to describe the benefit received from an item of revenue or income such as SALES, as distinct from the margin between buying and selling values, which is termed GROSS PROFIT, and the net gain remaining after the deduction of expenses, which is termed NET PROFIT. In this sense, gains are revenue or income whereas profits are gains less the relevant costs and expenses. As gains are that part of the calculation of profit which increases the capital liability, gains must also be recorded as credit (−) entries. If the gain was the sale of goods for £50,000, one side of the double entry would be a credit (−) in a Sales Account, as follows:

Dr (+)		SALES			Cr (−)
			Date	Cash for goods	£50,000

To reduce a minus (−) one must use a plus (+). As costs and expenses are that part of the calculation of profit which reduces the capital liability, costs and expenses must be recorded as debit (+) entries. If one account were to be used for the cost of the goods purchased for resale and the expenses involved, totalling £45,000, it would appear as follows:

Dr (+)		COSTS AND EXPENSES			Cr (−)
Date	Cash for goods plus expenses	£45,000			

If the gains, costs and expenses referred to above were to be entered directly into the Capital Account with the original investment, it would produce a net balance as between debit (+) and credit (−) of £24,000 credit (−) and appear as follows:

Dr (+)		CAPITAL A. BELL			Cr (−)
Date	Cash for goods plus expenses	£45,000	Date	Cash for original investment	£19,000
"	Balance carried down (increased capital)	24,000	"	Cash for goods sold	50,000
		£69,000			£69,000
			Date	Balance brought down (increased capital)	24,000

The illustration serves to show the necessity of recording costs and expenses as debits and gains as credits. It also shows that capital liability at the start of a trading period expressed as a credit (−), plus gains also expressed as credits (−), less costs and expenses expressed as debits (+) results in the capital liability at the close of the trading period:

Capital at start	£19,000 Credit (-)
Sales	50,000 Credit (-)
	69,000 Credit (-)
Costs and expenses	45,000 Debit (+)
Capital at close	24,000 Credit (-)

In practice, the various costs, expenses and gains are entered in separate accounts. The cost of goods purchased for resale is entered to the debit (+) of an account headed 'PURCHASES'. The sales value of goods sold is entered to the credit (−) of an account headed 'SALES'. The various expenses incurred are entered to the debit (+) of accounts which are headed according to the kind of expense which they record, such as rent, rates, light and heat, telephones, stationery, postage, etc. This grouping of expenses in separate accounts provides an automatic analysis which makes the total each kind of expense over a period of time immediately available.

The amount by which the gains exceed the costs and expenses is brought into the Capital Account as a net figure of profit, as shown in the second illustration of this account appearing on page 3. How this is achieved is explained in Chapters 2 and 6.

When a business incurs a liability it receives value in one form or another. When Mr Bell's business incurred the capital liability of £19,000 it received £19,000 in money, an asset which, as previously shown, was recorded as a debit (+) in the Cash Account:

Dr (+)	CASH			Cr (-)
Date	Capital	£19,000		

When a business parts with money it either reduces a liability or receives in exchange value in one form or another. When a business parts with value, whatever form the value takes, it receives value in exchange which, usually, takes the form of money or the right to receive money from its debtors.

If cash was received in exchange for the goods sold and cash was paid away in exchange for the value represented by the expenses and the goods purchased, the Cash Account in Mr Bell's business would have appeared as follows:

Dr (+)	CASH				Cr (-)
DATE	CAPITAL	£19,000	Date	Purchases of goods and expenses	£45,000
"	Sales	50,000	"	Balance carried down	24,000
		69,000			69,000
Date	Balance brought down	24,000			

This illustration and the illustration of the Capital Account appearing on page 4 show that, as a result of the transactions described, both the asset of cash and the capital liability were increased equally from £19,000 to £24,000, because a profit was made from the sale, for more than their cost, of the goods purchased and the expenses involved. If the business had parted with the value in the goods and expenses, for less than their cost, a loss would have been made and both the asset of cash and the capital liability would have been equally reduced instead of increased.

As previously stated, every transaction described in the accounts has two opposite entries of equal amount, one of which is a debit (+) and the other a credit (−). The accounting equation remains true irrespective of any change which takes place in the total net assets and the capital liability:

	£
Asset of Cash	24,000 (debit +)
Capital Liability	24,000 (credit -)
	NIL

In the accounts, profit or loss is measured by reference to the costs, expenses and gains, and related to the increase or decrease in the capital liability which is treated as a credit (−). Profit or loss is also reflected in the increase or decrease in the net total of assets which are treated as debit (+):

Cash at close	£24,000 Debit (+)
Cash at start	19,000 Debit (+)
Increase in assets	5,000 Debit (+)

INCREASE IN CAPITAL = INCREASE IN NET ASSETS = PROFIT

DECREASE IN CAPITAL = DECREASE IN NET ASSETS = LOSS

It must be remembered, however, that an increase in capital and net assets resulting from an INVESTMENT of capital in a business is not profit, and must not be treated as a gain; also, that a reduction of capital and net assets as a result of a WITHDRAWAL of capital, or profit made, is not loss, and must not be treated as an expense.

Profit or loss is also measured by reference to a period of time, or trading, and the accounts of a business must show how much has been made or lost during any given period. The costs, expenses and gains must, therefore, be related or apportioned to the specific period within which they have been expended or gained.

At the time when money is paid away, or a commitment is made to pay money, the value which is received in exchange is an asset, or possession. As soon as any part of the value received is used up, that part becomes an expense which must be taken into account in the calculation of profit or loss. Any unused portion of the value received which is carried forward remains an asset.

A cost or expense is that part of whatever value received its title signifies, which must be set against gains in a given period of trading for one or both of the following reasons:

(*a*) It has been used up in purchasing, producing, preparing for sale, selling, or distributing those goods or services which have been sold and delivered to clients during the period.

(*b*) It has been used up as a result of the passage of time.

An asset is that part of value received which, at any point in time, remains to be used up in future sales or as a result of the future passage of time.

If, in a given period of trading, a business has purchased goods costing £1,000 and sold half of them, the cost of goods to be set against the revenue from sales for that period is £500. The £500 worth of goods remaining on hand for future sales is an asset and will remain an asset until it is sold.

If, in a period of six months' trading, a business has paid £500 for its accommodation for a period of twelve months from the first day of the period, the expense to be set against gains for the six month period is £250. The remaining £250 worth of rent to be used up after the last day of the six month period is an asset which will continue to be consumed with the future passage of time.

The methods used in the accounts to carry forward from one trading period to the next the goods purchased but not sold are explained in Chapters 5 and 6. In the examples illustrated in Chapter 6, the expenses incurred by Mr Bell's business have been treated as completely used up within their respective trading periods. The treatment required to adjust expenses to the periods within which they are consumed is left to a later stage of study. The object here is to clarify the relationship between assets and expenses or costs, and the logic in recording both with debit (+) entries.

A debit (+) records EITHER the acquisition or increase of an asset, expense or cost, OR the elimination or reduction of a liability or gain.

A credit (–) records EITHER the creation or increase of a liability or gain, OR the elimination or reduction of an asset, expense or cost.

If, upon receiving the capital in cash, the first transaction entered into consisted of spending £500 in respect of rent for accommodation in business premises for a period of twelve months, the accounts would appear as follows:

Dr (+)		CASH			Cr (-)
JAN 1	CAPITAL	£19,000	Jan 1	Rent	£500

Dr (+)		CAPITAL	A. BELL		Cr (-)
			JAN 1	CASH	£19,000

Dr (+)		RENT			Cr (-)
Jan 1	Cash	£500			

The credit (–) entry made in the Cash Account recorded the reduction in the value of this asset and the debit (+) entry made in the Rent Account recorded the value received.

If, at the same time, the next transaction was the expenditure of £300 on office fixtures such as a desk and chairs, the accounts would then appear as follows:

Dr (+)		CASH			Cr (-)
JAN 1	CAPITAL	£19,000	JAN 1	RENT	£500
			" "	Office fixtures	£300

Dr (+)		CAPITAL	A. BELL		Cr (-)
			JAN 1	CASH	£19,000

Dr (+)		RENT			Cr (-)
JAN 1	CASH	£500			

Dr (+)		OFFICE FIXTURES			Cr (-)
Jan 1	Cash	£300			

The credit (–) entry made in the Cash Account recorded a further reduction in the value of this asset and the debit (+) entry made in the Office Fixtures Account recorded the acquisition of that asset.

As at the 1st January, although changes took place as a result of the transactions described, the total net value received remained equal to the capital liability:

	Debit (+)	Credit (-)	£
Cash	£18,200		£18,200 (+)
Rent	500		500 (+)
Office fixtures	300		300 (+)
Capital		£19,000	19,000 (-)
	£19,000	£19,000	NIL

On the 31st December of that year, the £500 rent would have been fully expended and set off against gains. If there were no gains it would have become a loss and would be set off against the capital liability. Assuming there were no gains, nor other transactions, during the year, the position at the end of the year would be:

	Debit (+)	Credit (-)	£
Assets:			
Office fixtures	£ 300		£ 300 (+)
Cash	18,200		18,200 (+)
Capital		£18,500	18,500 (-)
	£18,500	£18,500	NIL

The following summarises the principles so far explained, classifies the main kinds of assets and liabilities, and describes how the state of affairs of a business at the close of a trading period is displayed in a balance sheet.

Debits record Assets of which one may say there are three main kinds:

(i) Possessions NOT ACQUIRED FOR RESALE but FOR RETENTION AND USE in the business. These are called FIXED ASSETS because they tie up the money spent on them. (Premises, furniture, fixtures, plant and machinery are examples.)

(ii) Possessions being money, or items such as goods held for resale and debts receivable which are circulating into money flowing inwards. These are called CURRENT ASSETS because they are currently to be turned into money (realised).

(iii) Possessions in name only (nominal)* being costs and expenses to be resold, recharged or recovered from clients, either by inclusion in the selling prices for goods sold or by an independent charge. (Rent paid, wages, insurance costs, telephone calls and stationery expenses are examples.) These are not CALLED assets. They are eliminated by deduction from gains, mainly revenue from the sale of goods, in the calculation of the liability of the business to its proprietors in respect of the net profit made. They are called COSTS AND EXPENSES or REVENUE EXPENDITURE.

Therefore, DEBITS record, as one of the two aspects of each transaction, either an asset, expense or loss.

* See page 20, chapter 2.

Credits record Liabilities of which one may again say there are three main kinds:

(i) The capital of a business which is the amount of its liability to its proprietors. It is called CAPITAL.
(ii) Debts payable OTHER THAN liability to the proprietors. These are circulating into money flowing outwards. They are called CURRENT LIABILITIES when they are CURRENTLY to be turned into an outflow of money.
(iii) Gains (mainly the selling value of goods sold) which, after being reduced by the costs and expenses, become the liability of the business to its proprietor in respect of the net profit made. These are not CALLED liabilities. They exist in name only (nominal*) and when reduced to net profit as a liability to the proprietor, become an addition to CAPITAL.

Therefore, CREDITS record, as one of the two aspects of each transaction, either a liability, gain or profit.

In accounting, the term 'CURRENTLY' normally means 'DURING THE TWELVE MONTHS FOLLOWING THE END OF THE LAST PERIOD OF TRADING'.

In accounting, the term 'PREMISES' is used to indicate land and buildings for which the freehold has been bought and no rent is payable, or for which, when leased, a lump sum premium has been paid in addition to which rent is payable. The purchase price of freehold premises and the premium paid for leasehold premises are treated as fixed assets (capital expenditure) but rent is treated as an expense (revenue expenditure).

Net profit increases and net loss decreases the liability of a business to its proprietor. The following illustrates the foregoing principles, showing the position at the end of a period of trading.

			DEBITS (+) (Assets)	CREDITS (-) (Liabilities)
			£	£
CAPITAL (Amount invested by the proprietors)				19,000 (-)
NET PROFIT (An addition to CAPITAL)				
Sales	£50,000 (Credit)-			
Costs & expenses	£45,000 (Debit) +			5,000 (-)
INCREASED CAPITAL				24,000 (-)
FIXED ASSETS		£		
Premises		15,000 (+)		
Plant & Machinery		4,000 (+)		
Fixtures & fittings		2,000 (+)		
Motor vans		2,000 (+)	23,000(+)	
CURRENT ASSETS				
Stock (Goods held for resale)		11,000 (+)		
Debtors (Money due from clients)		7,000 (+)		
Cash held at bank		990 (+)		
Loose cash held on premises		10 (+)	19,000(+)	
CURRENT LIABILITIES				
Creditors (Money owing to suppliers)				18,000 (-)
			42,000(+)	42,000 (-)

* See page 20, chapter 2.

It can be seen that the liability to the proprietors is represented as a credit of £24,000 arrived at by adding the net profit made to the original investment. This is equal to the remaining NET assets, the latter being the total of all the assets less the total of all liabilities OTHER THAN THE LIABILITY TO THE PROPRIETORS. This is illustrated by rearranging the above figures in vertical form as a balance sheet.

BALANCE SHEET AS AT ....19..

	£	
CURRENT ASSETS (debits)	19,000	+
CURRENT LIABILITIES (credits)	18,000	-
NET CURRENT ASSETS (debit)	1,000	+
FIXED ASSETS (debits)	23,000	+
TOTAL NET ASSETS (debit)	24,000	+
Represented by, financed by, or equal to:		
CAPITAL (credit)		
Original Investment (credit)	19,000	-
Net profit (credit)	5,000	-
	24,000	-

It should be clear from the foregoing that the total of all debits (assets) must be equal to the total of all credits (liabilities). In the final analysis, assets and liabilities are two opposite ways of expressing the same entity: on the one hand the monetary value of the net possessions (net assets) and on the other hand, the amount of the liability of the business to its proprietor (capital).

In traditional form the figures in the above example would be presented as follows:

BALANCE SHEET AS AT .... 19..

	£	£		£	£
CAPITAL			FIXED ASSETS		
Original Investment	19,000		Premises	15,000	
Add net profit	5,000	24,000	Plant & M/cy	4,000	
			Fixtures & Ftgs	2,000	
			Motor vans	2,000	23,000
CURRENT LIABILITIES					
Creditors		18,000	CURRENT ASSETS		
			Stock	11,000	
			Debtors	7,000	
			Cash at Bank	990	
			Cash in hand	10	19,000
		42,000			42,000

Traditionally, the assets and liabilities in this form of balance sheet, which IS NOT AN ACCOUNT but merely a LIST of the balances in the accounts, are placed on the opposite sides to those on which they appear in the accounts.

However, the confusion which this can cause in the early stages of study is avoided when the vertical form previously shown is used.

In the continental Common Market countries and the U.S.A., the recognised traditional form of balance sheet is listed with the assets on the left side and the liabilities on the right side, i.e. on the same sides as they appear in the accounts. Unless this form of presentation is recognised as acceptable in the U.K., the vertical or traditional form as per examples illustrated should be used, subject to any instructions which may be contained in a question and the requirements, if any, of the relevant examining board.

The grand totals at the foot of the traditional form of balance sheet have no significance other than to show that the GROSS total of the assets is equal to the total of the capital liability AND ALL OTHER LIABILITIES.

The student must distinguish between TOTAL ASSETS (£42,000 in the example) and Total NET Assets (£24,000 in the example.)

The figure of total assets in the traditional form of balance sheet represents the total cost value of all the assets in the business irrespective of whether or not they have been paid for. It includes the debtors representing money which cannot be used until it is received and cash at bank and in hand representing idle money.

In certain circumstances, the total assets are described as the ASSETS EMPLOYED although, in the early stages of study the terms ASSETS EMPLOYED and CAPITAL EMPLOYED are usually taken to mean the total NET ASSETS, which amount is equal to the capital liability. The latter terms have other interpretations which are dealt with in an advanced study of accounting.

If the total of the CURRENT liabilities be greater than the total of the CURRENT assets, there is a deficiency of NET current assets or a NET current LIABILITY. This is a serious position for a business as it indicates that there is not sufficient money flowing inwards, even if the stock of unsold goods can be quickly turned into money, to enable the business to pay its creditors in full.

If the total of liabilities other than the capital liability is greater than the total assets, there is a deficiency of total net assets or net worth. This means that the business has insufficient total assets to cover its liabilities to the outside world even after the owner's investment (Capital) has been reduced to NIL. It means that the losses of capital invested are greater than the total amount invested. In such circumstances the Capital Account shows a debit (+) balance indicating that instead of the business having a liability to the owner, the owner has a liability to the business and that to cover the liabilities of the business to the outside world the owner must pay into the business the amount of the deficiency. A business in this state of affairs is described as being insolvent.

The balance of an account is the net result of the entries which have been made therein. If the total of the debit (+) entries is greater than the total of the credit (−) entries, the difference is a debit (+) balance. If the total of the credit (−) entries is greater than the total of the debit (+) entries, the difference is a credit (−) balance.

In order to complete a balance sheet, the balances in all the accounts must be calculated as at the date of the balance sheet. In order that there shall remain a record of such balances in the accounts, an operation called BALANCING OFF is carried out. This replaces, in each account, all the figures appearing therein, up to and including the date of the balance sheet, with a single figure showing their net result. This figure represents both the balance at the close of one period of accounting and the balance at the start of the following period of accounting.

Balancing off can also be done at any time when a complete list of the balances in the accounts is required in order to ascertain the overall state of the affairs of a business. Balances can be carried down in any particular group of accounts at any time when they are required for a special purpose such as the calculation from the accounts of the clients (debtors) of the total amount of money owing to the business. A balance may be carried down in an account at any time when the net result of the entries in respect of a particular item is required, such as the amount of money in the bank which is calculated by balancing off the Cash Account.

As with every other move or adjustment which is made in the accounts, the balancing off of each account must be done with a double entry. To transfer a debit (+) balance from one period to the next, the period ended must be credited and the new period debited. To transfer a credit (−) balance from one period to the next, the period ended must be debited and the new period credited.

The entry in the period ended is described as BALANCE CARRIED DOWN. The entry in the new period is described as BALANCE BROUGHT DOWN. The former is entered against the date of the last day of the period ended and the latter is entered against the date of the first day of the new period.

Sufficient space is left between the two periods to permit the insertion of the totals of the debits and credits for the period ended. One of these includes the balance CARRIED down and they will, therefore, be equal in amount and cancel each other out.

The two totals are entered, one on each side of the account, horizontally opposite to each other, with a single line ruled immediately above each one and a double line ruled immediately below each one. They indicate that all the entries above them are closed off.

For examples, reference should be made to the illustrations appearing on pages 4 and 5 of this chapter and on pages 44 and 45 of Chapter 6.

Good workmanship must be used in producing accounts and in presenting answers to questions in exercises and examinations.

Each set of accounts must be headed with the name of the business with which it is concerned.

Although exercises and examination answers necessitate the presentation of accounts underneath each other on sheets of paper, it should be remembered that each individual account is a separate entity which must contain all the information which is relevant to that account. The year of the dates must be recorded in every single account. Accounts cannot be combined or added together except by transferring their contents or balances to another account such as the Trading and Profit and Loss Account.* Figures in every account should be headed with the relevant currency sign such as the '£' although, in practice, this is often omitted except when producing revenue accounts, balance sheets, statements and calculations.

Dates are of the utmost importance. Papers ruled for accounts provide a pair of columns for dates. The first of the pair should be used for the month, which may be

* See page 20, chapter 2.

abbreviated, and the second for the day. The year should be entered as a heading across the date columns and need not be repeated until it changes.

Unnecessary spaces must not be left between entries in accounts. The only permissible spaces are those which are unavoidable because there are more debit entries than credit entries or more credit entries than debit entries.

Names of accounts should be centred and need not be suffixed with the word 'Account'.

Each single entry in an account is described, in the column provided for particulars next to the date, by writing in the name of the other account in which the opposite part of the double entry is made. It follows that the name of an account is never used to describe an entry in that same account.

The old custom of prefixing debit entries with the word 'To' and credit entries with the word 'By' is no longer followed.

Extreme care must be taken when balancing off. Having added the entries in each side of an account to calculate its balance and having entered the balance carried down, the totals of each side should be re-cast to make sure that they agree and that the balance is correct. Never forget to insert the balance brought down and check that it is the same as the balance carried down.

For the names of accounts and headings for calculations and statements, if there is a choice and so far as is practicable, the student is advised to conform with those used in the question which is being answered. In practice, of course, they depend upon the requirements of the particular business in which they are used. Calculations and statements are best presented in ordinary mathematical or vertical form unless the question specifically calls for account form.

When listing a column of figures in or apart from the accounts, keep the units, tens, hundreds, etc. underneath each other in straight upright lines. This makes the figures easy to read, add or subtract and leads to clarity and accuracy. It is also helpful to insert a comma to separate the thousands from the hundreds.

The abbreviations 'c/d' and 'b/d' must not be confused one with the other and are best placed in the folio column. In practice, when all double entries have been completed, the folio column against each single entry in the accounts must contain either the identification reference of the other account in which its opposite entry is recorded to complete the double entry, or one of the abbreviations for 'carried down', 'brought down', 'carried forward', 'brought forward' or 'contra'. This practice lessens the risk of only one side of a double entry being recorded. A blank space in the folio column against an entry is easily seen. In answers to exercises and examination questions it is generally not practicable to insert in the folio columns the account references. However, 'c/d' and 'b/d' should never be omitted against balances, nor should 'c/f' and 'b/f' be omitted against totals carried forward and brought forward.

The folio column is shown in the following illustration and its use clarified in Chapter 6.

The term 'contra', meaning against, and abbreviated to 'C', is used when both sides of a double entry appear in the same account. An example is when separate columns, side by side on both sides, are used for cash in hand and cash at bank in one account to record movements of money in the form of notes and coin between a business and its bank. To illustrate this, the double entries for the sale of goods for £200 in notes

1 January 19. ., the payment into the bank of £100 of the notes 2 January 19. . and the withdrawal from the bank of £50 in notes 3 January 19. . would be as follows:

SALES A/c.ref: NL/6

			Folio		19..			Folio	
					Jan	1	Cash	CB/1	200.-

CASH BOOK A/c.ref: CB/1

19..			Folio	Cash	Bank	19..			Folio	Cash	Bank
Jan	1	Sales	NL/6	200.-		Jan	2	Bank	C	100.-	
"	2	Cash	C		100.-	"	3	Cash	C		50.-
"	3	Bank	C	50.-		"	3	Balances	c/d	150.-	50.-
				250.-	100.-					250.-	100.-
"	4	Balances b/d		150.-	50.-						

The above example should be carefully studied and thoroughly understood.

This method of separating cash in hand from cash at bank in the same account is only used in special circumstances. The usual practice is to pay ALL cash received straight into the bank, debiting it to a Cash Account, and to withdraw from the bank only small amounts of notes and coin which are debited to a separate account called PETTY CASH, to record the asset of cash in hand, and credited to the Cash Account to record the reduction in the asset of cash at bank. All payments by the business are, so far as is possible, made direct from the bank, using cheques or other methods available for this purpose, and credited to the Cash Account to record the reduction in the asset of cash at bank. Small payments which have to be made in notes and coin from cash in hand are credited to the Petty Cash Account to record the reduction in that asset. This method ensures that the handling of physical cash is kept to the minimum possible amount, which has many advantages. The examples illustrated in Chapter 6 should be studied.

THE MATHEMATICAL FORMULA FOR THE DOUBLE ENTRY SYSTEM OF ACCOUNTING
APPLIED TO THE EXAMPLES USED IN THE PRECEDING TEXT

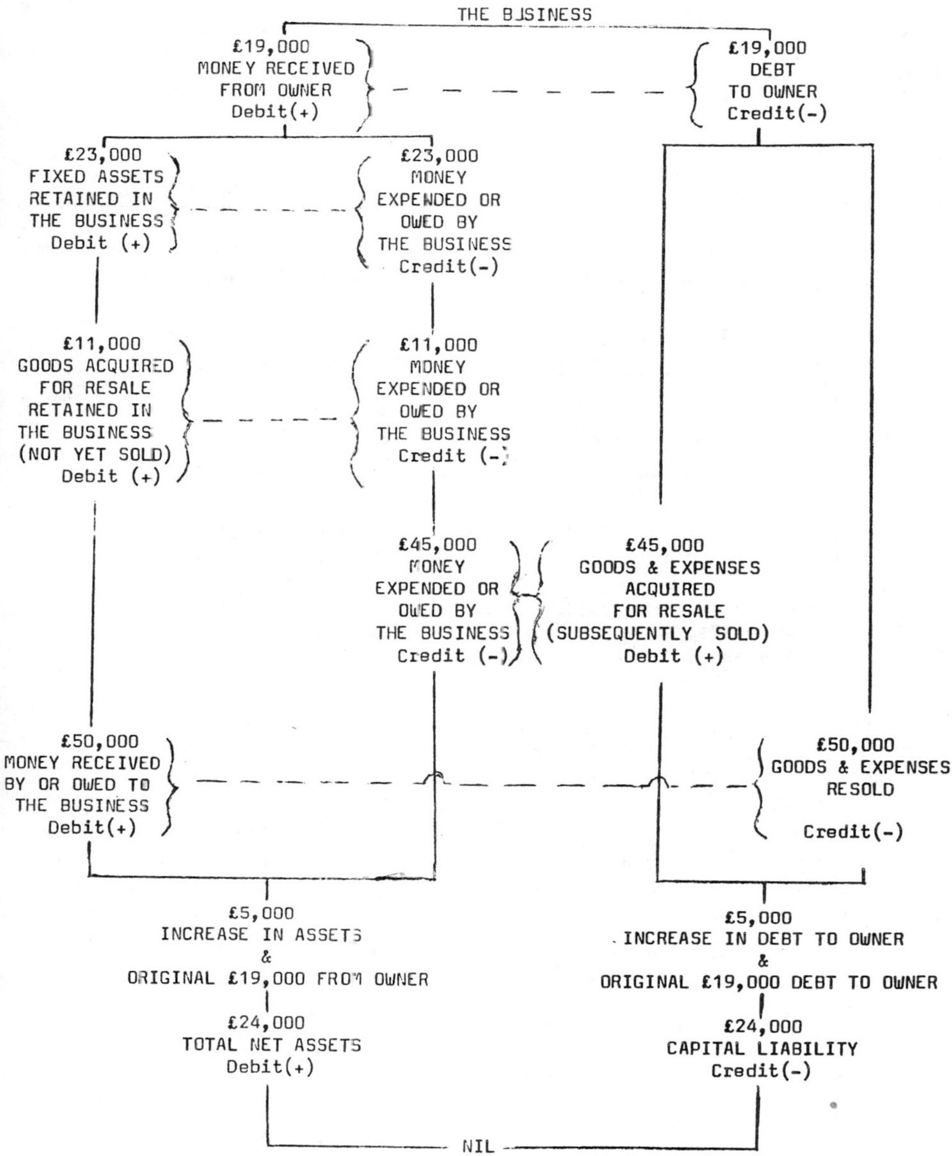

The £24,000 worth of NET assets is made up as follows:

			£
FIXED ASSETS			23,000 (+)
STOCK OF GOODS UNSOLD			11,000 (+)
			34,000 (+)
MONEY:-		£	
From owner		19,000 (+)	
From sale of goods and expenses		50,000 (+)	
		69,000 (+)	
	£		
Expended on fixed assets	23,000 (-)		
Expended on goods unsold	11,000 (-)		
Expended on goods & expenses resold	45,000 (-)	79,000 (-)	10,000 (-)
			24,000 (+)

The deficiency of money belonging to the business is made up as follows:

	£
CASH AT BANK	990 (+)
CASH IN HAND	10 (+)
OWING TO THE BUSINESS BY THE DEBTORS	7,000 (+)
	8,000 (+)
OWING BY THE BUSINESS TO THE CREDITORS	18,000 (-)
Deficiency	10,000 (-)

The money which has provided the means by which the business acquired the fixed assets and the stock of goods, totalling £34,000, is made up as follows:

		£
INVESTED BY OWNER		19,000
BORROWED FROM THE CREDITORS		18,000
FROM PROFIT MADE		5,000
		42,000
	£	
Less: LENT TO THE DEBTORS	7,000	
IDLE MONEY (Cash at bank & in hand)	1,000	8,000
		34,000

To show why, in spite of a starting capital in cash of £19,000 and cash received from profits of £5,000, the balance of cash at bank and in hand at close is only £1,000, a statement of the sources and applications of cash (cash flow) can be completed as follows:

STATEMENT OF CHANGES IN CASH POSITION

		£
Cash at bank and in hand at start		19,000
Profits earned		5,000
Borrowed from creditors		18,000
	£	42,000
Expended on Fixed Assets	23,000	
" " goods unsold	11,000	
Lent to Debtors	7,000	41,000
Cash at bank and in hand at close		1,000

Note that the expenditure on goods and expenses resold (£45,000) and the revenue from the sale of those goods and expenses (£50,000) have been set off against each other and shown as one figure of profit (£5,000).

ORDER OF LISTING ASSETS AND LIABILITIES ON A BALANCE SHEET. The order in which balances are listed and grouped is sometimes called marshalling.

In the balance sheet, the main object is to present the information which it contains in such a way as to make it easy to read and understand – to leave as little rearrangement of balances and further calculations for the full interpretation of its contents as may be possible. The vertical form lends itself to this purpose more readily than the double-sided form, particularly when it shows the net current assets, or net current liability, as the case may be, already calculated. The total of each group of assets and liabilities must be shown as a separate sub-total of the balance sheet.

The secondary object is standardisation. The establishment of a standard order enables individual balances and groups of balances to be found quickly on any balance sheet. It also makes easy comparison of the balance sheet at the close of one trading period with those at the close of previous periods in the same business and those of other businesses.

For fixed assets, the order of listing depends upon the length of time they are expected to remain in the business. Those which are most permanent are placed first and those which are least permanent are placed last. Land and buildings have great permanence whereas motor vehicles have a comparatively short life.

For current assets, the order of listing is governed by the time which is expected to pass before realisation takes place. The asset which will take the longest to turn into cash is placed first and cash itself is placed last. In normal circumstances, trading is on credit terms and stock has to be sold before debtors are created; debtors have to make payment to the business before cash is realised.

The Capital is the one liability which stands alone, separate and distinct from all assets and other liabilities. It is equal and opposite to and cannot, therefore, be part of the assets and liabilities which make up the total net assets or net worth. In the vertical form of balance sheet this separation is made obvious whereas in the double-sided form it tends to be obscured by being linked with the liabilities to the outside world. In thinking or speaking of the liabilities of a business, one should exclude the capital liability to the owner.

For the liabilities to the outside world, the general rule is to list them in the opposite order to that in which they must be met or discharged, that is paid off. This method only has much significance in the double-sided form of balance sheet, in which the capital is listed first and the liabilities to the outside world follow. Even in the double-sided form of balance sheet, except when dealing with the current liabilities, the method is not of significance to the student until such time as he is introduced to long term and medium term liabilities which are listed in that order between the capital and the current liabilities. The only current liabilities which the student has to cope with at this stage of study are the creditors and a bank overdraft. The order in which these are listed is not important. It is the part they play in the calculation of the monetary position, as will be seen in Chapter 3, which is important.

There are no absolute rules as to how a balance sheet must be presented or laid out. As studies advance, and in practice, alternative forms of presentation will be met with. For instance, fixed assets are sometimes listed before the current assets. Meanwhile, the forms of presentation already illustrated, and the general rules explained above, should be adhered to.

EXERCISES

1. Explain, briefly but clearly, what you understand by each of the following accounting concepts:

   (*a*) Business Entity
   (*b*) Duality
   (*c*) Management

2. A. Jax started a business 1 January 1970. During the period ended 8 January 1970 the following transactions were completed:

   1970
   Jan. 1 Received £5,000 from Mr Jax as starting capital
   Jan. 2 Paid £1,000 for goods for resale.
   Jan. 4 Sold the goods purchased and received £1,500 for them.
   Jan. 8 Paid £200 for the expenses incurred during the period.

   You are required to:

   (*a*) open the following accounts and make therein the double entries necessary to record the transactions:

   Cash Account. Capital Account. Purchases Account.
   Sales Account. Expenses Account.

   (*b*) calculate in vertical (tabular) form the profit made during the period ended 8 January 1970.
   (*c*) calculate in vertical (tabular) form the increase in capital which has taken place during the period.
   (*d*) compile a balance sheet as at 8 January 1970 in traditional form.

3. J. Besby commenced in business 1 March 1971.

   (*a*) Open the required business accounts and make therein the necessary entries to record the following transactions which were completed during the first week of trading:

   1971
   March 1 Received £3,000 in cash as capital from J. Besby.
   March 1 Paid £20 rent for premises for one week.
   March 2 Paid £150 for office fixtures.
   March 3 Paid £900 for goods for resale.
   March 4 Received £1,200 from the sale of the goods purchased.
   March 5 Paid £50 in settlement of the general expenses incurred to date.

   (*b*) From the information contained in the accounts, make two statements in vertical (tabular) form, one of which is to show the make-up and total net value of the assets, and the other is to show your calculation of the counterbalancing capital liability to J. Besby, both as at 5 March 1971.

4. (*a*) From the balances listed below, which were extracted from the accounts of the business of A. Glyder as at 30 June 1971, compile the balance sheet as at that date, in conventional form, and redraft it in vertical form for management:

	£
Capital (including profit made to date)	6,683
Cash at bank	462
Machinery	3,261
Creditors	7,432
Motor Vans	2,500
Debtors	5,666
Office fixtures	942
Cash in hand	34
Stock of unsold goods	1,250

(*b*) Show your calculation of the profit made since the original investment, which amounted to £5,000, was introduced.

CHAPTER 2

Accounts

In the illustration on page 9 the sales, costs and expenses are placed together with the remaining assets and liabilities to show how they produce the net profit which is included with the liabilities. In practice, these gains, costs and expenses are not *detailed* in the balance sheet, but shown therein as one item of net profit. Instead, for the purpose of calculating the net profit, they are brought together by transferring them from their individual accounts into one final account. If the gains (credits) in this account total more than the costs and expenses (debits), the difference (balance) is the net profit. If the total of the debits exceeds the total of the credits, the resultant debit balance is a net loss. The former increases the liability of the business to its proprietors and the latter decreases it. This final account is called THE TRADING AND PROFIT AND LOSS ACCOUNT. It is divided into two sections, the first of which is called THE TRADING ACCOUNT and the second THE PROFIT AND LOSS ACCOUNT. They are also called REVENUE ACCOUNTS or Income Statements.

The Trading Account is used to calculate the GROSS PROFIT which is the margin of profit between the sales value of the goods sold and the COST of the goods sold, from which the expenses of running the business have to be recovered.

The Profit and Loss Account is used to calculate the net profit remaining after the expenses of running the business have been deducted from the gross profit.

In addition to the particular name given to each account to indicate what it records it is also placed in a type-group to indicate what *kind* of account it is. The types are:

THE CAPITAL ACCOUNT which is used to record the liability of the business to its proprietors. This is a personal account.
PERSONAL ACCOUNTS in which monies owing to the business by its clients and monies owing by the business to its suppliers are recorded.
REAL ACCOUNTS in which the real (physical) possessions such as cash, stock of goods for trading and fixed assets are recorded.
NOMINAL ACCOUNTS for gains, costs and expenses.
REVENUE ACCOUNTS into which the gains, costs, expenses etc. are transferred from the nominal accounts and in which the profits (or losses) are calculated. (The Trading and Profit and Loss Accounts.)

It must be emphasised that the BALANCE SHEET IS NOT AN ACCOUNT but a statement or list of the final balances in the accounts after the revenue accounts have been made up. It sets out the balances remaining open in the accounts to show the financial state of affairs at a particular point in time.

The balances in nominal accounts are used to calculate profit or loss and capital liability, whereas the balances in real accounts and personal accounts are used to calculate the total net assets or net worth.

Items of stationery, such as letterheads, various kinds of forms, ledger sheets, punches, staplers, pens, envelopes, pins, paper clips, erasers, typewriter ribbons, carbon papers, and similar accessories are normally bought as required for current use, and are treated as expense which is recoverable in the current sales. The balance in the Stationery Account is used in the calculation of profit or loss and capital liability and is, therefore, nominal.

The Cash Account is a real account irrespective of whether its balance is debit (+) representing money at the bank or credit (−) representing an overdraft, that is the amount by which monies paid out from the bank are greater than the monies paid into the bank. Whichever of these the balance may be, it is not used in the calculation of profit or loss and capital liability but in the calculation of the total net assets or net worth.

The dual nature of transactions must not be lost sight of. Each account records only one side of a transaction. A transaction has two sides. These may be one of several alternative pairs:

(*a*) REAL and REAL, as when cash is exchanged for a fixed asset.
(*b*) REAL and PERSONAL, as when a fixed asset is bought on credit terms.*
(*c*) REAL and NOMINAL, as when purchases and sales are made, and expenses incurred, on a cash basis.
(*d*) PERSONAL and NOMINAL, as when purchases and sales are made, and expenses are incurred, on credit terms.*

FINAL ACCOUNTS This term refers to the revenue accounts AND THE BALANCE SHEET. It is a little misleading in so far as the Balance Sheet is concerned. Whilst the Balance Sheet does set out the final results of a period of trading according to the calculations made in the accounts proper, as previously stated, it is not an 'account' within the normal meaning of the term in accounting language.

It should be noted that each item of gain, cost or expense, *at the time of the transaction*, is recorded in its appropriate nominal account, and periodically, when the final accounts are made up, the net totals or balances are eliminated from the nominal accounts by transfers to the revenue accounts.

The real account for cash at bank, because of the numerous entries therein and consequent bulkiness, is kept separately, and is known as the CASH ACCOUNT or CASH BOOK.

The real account for loose cash kept on hand for small items of expenditure, for the payment of which cheques are not suitable, is for convenience kept separately. This is called the PETTY CASH ACCOUNT or PETTY CASH BOOK.

The remaining real accounts, the Capital Account and the revenue accounts, are usually grouped together in one ledger. This is the PRIVATE LEDGER.

The nominal accounts are usually grouped together in another ledger called the NOMINAL LEDGER, the personal accounts of clients (debtors) in a separate SALES LEDGER, and the personal accounts of suppliers (creditors) in a separate PURCHASES LEDGER or BOUGHT LEDGER as it is sometimes called.

* See chapter 3.

In some cases the private ledger accounts and the nominal ledger accounts are combined in one GENERAL LEDGER. In some instances the clients' accounts are so numerous as to require more than one sales ledger.

When accounting is performed manually, a ledger consists of either a bound book or a loose leaf binder containing a number of separate accounts in which a proper record of transactions is kept. When more modern methods such as 'one-writing' systems, keyboard accounting machine systems and punched card accounting systems are adopted, transactions may be recorded on loose sheets or cards which may be kept in special trays, boxes or cabinets. The study of such systems of accounting is a specialised one which must be preceded by a clear understanding of the manual system to which the instruction in this book is confined. The same principles must be applied, and the same objects achieved, whatever system of working the accounts may be adopted.

Businesses marketing equipment for 'one-writing' methods and machines for mechanised bookkeeping and accounting employ specialists to examine manual systems in use, suggest how they may be improved, and give initial instruction to their customers' personnel as to how to work the new systems which the use of their equipment or machines makes possible.

It is worth noting that some accounts are both nominal and real. The Purchases Account, the Sales Account and the Stock Account are nominal in that they record items which have been taken into account by transfers to the revenue accounts in calculating profits, and real in that they are also records of goods which are physical possessions. The Purchases Account records the cost of goods acquired for resale, the Sales Account records the selling value of the goods parted with, and the Stock Account records the cost of goods remaining in possession of the business on the date at which the revenue accounts are made up. In practice the purchases and sales accounts are treated as nominal and the stock account as real.

It is also worth noting that the Cash Account is both real and personal. It is real in that it records money possessed and personal in that it records the debt existing between the business and its banker. It serves a dual purpose; firstly to record the flow of money between the business, its proprietor and the outside world, and secondly to record the flow of money between the business and its bank. As the two records are identical, only one account is used for both purposes. In practice it is treated as real.

Reference should be made to Chapter 5 for instruction as to the methods used in the accounts to arrive at the cost of the goods purchased and resold which, in the following diagram, is included in the total costs and expenses, and the cost of the goods purchased but not resold which, in the following diagram, is shown as stock.

The individual transactions, accounts and double entries therein, from which the diagram has been constructed, are described and illustrated in detail in Chapter 6.

BASIC FRAMEWORK OF ACCOUNTS

THE BUSINESS

THE ACCOUNTS

CASH (Real Account)

Dr (+)		Cr (-)	
(A)	19,000	(B)	23,000
(H)	43,000	(C)	11,000
		(D)	26,960
		(E)	50
		(v)	990
	62,000		62,000
(v)	990		

PETTY CASH (Real Account)

Dr (+)		Cr-	
(E)	50	(G)	40
		(w)	10
	50		50
(w)	10		

CREDITORS (Personal Accounts)

Dr (+)		Cr (-)	
		(F)	18,000

DEBTORS (Personal Accounts)

Dr (+)		Cr (-)	
(I)	7,000		

FIXED ASSETS (Real Accounts)

Dr (+)		Cr (-)	
(B)	23,000		

STOCK (Real Account)

Dr (+)		Cr(-)	
(C)	11,000		

CAPITAL (Personal Account)

Dr (+)		Cr (-)	
		(A)	19,000
		(z)	5,000
			24,000

COSTS & EXPENSES (Nominal Accounts)

Dr (+)		Cr (-)	
(D)	26,960	(x)	45,000
(F)	18,000		
(G)	40		
	45,000		45,000

GAINS (Nominal Accounts)

Dr (+)		Cr (-)	
(y)	50,000	(H)	43,000
		(I)	7,000
	50,000		50,000

TRADING AND PROFIT AND LOSS (Revenue Account)

Dr (+)		Cr (-)	
(x)	45,000	(y)	50,000
(z)	5,000		
	50,000		50,000

THE FINAL BALANCES

TOTAL NET ASSETS

Stock	11,000(+)
Debtors	7,000(+)
Cash at bank	990(+)
Cash in hand	10(+)
	19,000(+)
Creditors	18,000(-)
Net Current Assets	1,000(+)
Fixed Assets	23,000(+)
TOTAL NET ASSETS	24,000(+)

CAPITAL LIABILITY

Original Investment	19,000(-)
Profit for period	5,000(-)
REVISED CAPITAL	24,000(-)

NIL

For the purposes of illustration only, the two parts of each of the double entries relating to transactions are linked with one of the reference letters A to H, and the two parts of each of the double entries representing the final moves in the accounts are linked with one of the reference letters v to z. The figures used are those illustrated, in balance sheet form, on page 10. As it is impracticable to show all the individual accounts which comprise the debtors, creditors, fixed assets, costs, expenses and gains in one complete picture, they are, in each case, shown in total in one account.

A description of what each pair of entries represents is given in the following key:

KEY TO DIAGRAM OF BASIC FRAMEWORK OF ACCOUNTS

	£
A..Capital introduced and paid into the business bank	19,000
B..Fixed assets bought with bank money	23,000
C..Goods purchased with bank money but not yet resold	11,000
D..Goods and expenses bought with bank money and resold ..	26,960
E..Cash withdrawn from bank for petty expenditure	50
F..Goods and expenses bought, resold, but not yet paid for by the business	18,000
G..Petty expenses paid for ex cash in hand and recovered in the gains	40
H..Goods and expenses sold for money paid into the bank ..	43,000
I..Goods and expenses sold but not yet paid for by the clients	7,000
v..Balance of cash at bank carried down	990
w..Balance of cash in hand carried down	10
x..Total costs and expenses transferred to the Trading and Profit and Loss Account	45,000
y..Total gains transferred to the Trading and Profit and Loss Account	50,000
z..Net profit transferred from the Profit and Loss Account to the Capital Account	5,000

The Mathematical Formula is operated in the accounts by means of double entries. The result which the operation of the Formula produces consists of the final balances in the accounts which are listed in the Balance Sheet.

EXERCISES

1. Describe the criteria by which one judges whether an account is real, nominal or personal and the role which the balance in each of these three kinds of account plays within the mathematical formula for accounting.
2. The following is a list of balances extracted from the business accounts of V. Sweet as at 30 September 1971, before any transfers were made from nominal accounts to the Trading and Profit and Loss Account:

Name of account	Kind of account	Debit(+) £	Credit(-) £
SALARIES............	......	3,129	
FREEHOLD PREMISES..	......	7.500	
BANK CHARGES	......	15	
CASH	......	495	
PURCHASES OF GOODS.	......	24,500	
POSTAGE	......	20	
PETTY CASH	......	5	
OFFICE FIXTURES ...	......	1,000	
TELEPHONE EXPENSES.	......	61	
SALES OF GOODS	......		30,000
RENT PAID	......	250	
MOTOR VANS	......	1,000	
PLANT	......	2,000	
SUNDRY DEBTORS	......	3,500	
SUNDRY CREDITORS ..	......		8,975
CAPITAL	......		

You are required to:

(*a*) calculate and insert the missing amount.
(*b*) insert the total of the debits and of the credits.
(*c*) state against each account whether it is real, nominal or personal.

CHAPTER 3

Cash and Credit Transactions

As has already been indicated on pages 4 & 5 of Chapter 1 and is further explained in Chapter 5, 'Purchases' and 'Sales' are terms which, in accounting, have special meanings and uses. This also applies to the terms 'CASH' and 'PETTY CASH'. In accounting, 'cash' is not confined to notes and coin. It includes all monies paid into or withdrawn from the bank account of the business, irrespective of whether it is in the form of loose cash, cheques, postal orders, money orders, credit transfers or other means of exchanging money. As, however, it is necessary to distinguish the loose money kept on hand from the money kept in the bank, it is usual to describe the former as 'PETTY CASH'. The interpretation given of 'CASH' still applies when it is used to indicate that goods sold or purchased have been paid for immediately the transaction took place. A 'CASH TRANSACTION' is one in respect of which payment IN ANY FORM is made AT THE TIME OF THE TRANSACTION.

The term 'CREDIT' also has special meanings and uses in accounting. It has already been shown that a credit in the books of a business is a credit entry in an account and represents a liability, gain or profit, as also does a credit balance. The term 'CREDIT' is also used to indicate that a period of time has been allowed within which payment for goods sold or purchased may be made. A transaction entered into on this basis is a 'CREDIT TRANSACTION'. Such a transaction is said to have been made on credit terms.

Students may find it helpful to distinguish between money POSSESSED and money OWNED. The money possessed is the total of the debit balances in the Cash Account and the Petty Cash Account. The money owned is the total possessed, plus the total monies owed by clients to the business (sundry debtors), less the total monies owed by the business (sundry creditors). When money is paid to the business by clients (debtors), the effect is to INCREASE the money POSSESSED, DECREASE the money owed to the business (debtors) but leave the money OWNED unchanged. When money is paid by the business to creditors, the effect is to reduce the amount POSSESSED, REDUCE the amount of money owed by the business (sundry creditors), but again leave the money OWNED unchanged.

When a CASH transaction is entered into with a client in respect of goods sold, the Cash Account is debited with the money received and the Sales Account is credited to record the gain. When, however, goods are sold on CREDIT terms, no money is received at the time when the transaction takes place so that whilst the Sales Account can be credited with the gain, the Cash Account cannot be debited with any money. Instead of the money POSSESSED being increased the money OWNED is increased by the creation of a debt payable TO the business. The client becomes a debtor to the business and the debit entry for this transaction is made in his personal account in the

Sales Ledger. In both cases the necessary double entry has been completed in the accounts. The receipt of money from the client at a later date has to be treated as a separate transaction also requiring a double entry. At the time when it is received, the Cash Account is debited and the debtor's account in the Sales Ledger is credited, thus increasing the money possessed decreasing the sundry debtors but leaving the monetary position unchanged

When a CASH transaction is entered into with a supplier in respect of goods purchased, the Cash Account is credited with the money paid away and the Purchases Account is debited to record the cost. When, however, goods are purchased on CREDIT terms, no money is paid away at the time when the transaction takes place, so that whilst the Purchases Account can be debited with the cost, the Cash Account cannot be credited with any money. Instead of the money POSSESSED being reduced the money OWNED is reduced by the creation of a debt payable BY the business. The supplier becomes a creditor of the business and the credit entry for this transaction is made in his personal account in the Purchases Ledger. In both cases the necessary double entry has been completed in the accounts. The payment of money to the supplier at a later date has to be treated as a separate transaction also requiring a double entry. At the time when the payment is made, the Cash Account is credited and the creditor's account in the Purchases Ledger is debited, thus decreasing the money possessed, decreasing the sundry creditors but leaving the monetary position unchanged.

It should be noted that the money possessed is only increased or decreased by the movement of money and that the money owned, i.e. the monetary position is only changed by the movement of value other than money. Sales create an increase in the monetary position. Purchases of goods or services, and all other expenditure, irrespective of whether the result of cash transactions or credit transactions, create a decrease in the monetary position.

It is very important for a business to know, preferably at least once a month, what the monetary position is, that is to say what the total net money owned amounts to. A business must, at all times, have sufficient money at its bank and flowing inwards from its debtors to provide the money which must flow outwards to its creditors, if it is not to get into financial difficulties. If money is also flowing inwards from sources other than the debtors, or flowing outwards in payment of liabilities other than the creditors, such items must also be taken into consideration in deciding what new commitments involving an outflow of money can be undertaken.

For examples of the treatment in the accounts of cash and credit transactions, the student should refer to pages 44 and 45 of Chapter 6.

The following illustration demonstrates the effects of payments, revenue and expenditure on the overall monetary position. It shows, reading from left to right, the changes which take place as each new transaction is booked.

It is interesting to see how much information can be deduced from these figures

(*a*) The total purchases of £1,250 exceeded the total sales of £450 by £800 and the overall monetary position was deteriorated by £800 from a surplus of £1,100 at start to a surplus of only £300 at close.

(*b*) The cash possessed was reduced from a surplus of £1,000 to deficiency of £50, necessitating borrowing.

	As at start	Debtors pay £200	Creditors are paid £300	Credit sales booked £400
	£	£	£	£
Cash at bank and in hand	1,000 (Dr)	1,200 (Dr)	900 (Dr)	900(Dr)
Sundry debtors	500 (Dr)	300 (Dr)	300 (Dr)	700(Dr)
	1,500 (Dr)	1,500 (Dr)	1,200 (Dr)	1,600(Dr)
Sundry creditors	400 (Cr)	400 (Cr)	100 (Cr)	100(Cr)
	1,100 (Dr)	1,100 (Dr)	1,100 (Dr)	1,500(Dr)

	Credit purchases booked £250	Cash sales booked £50	Cash purchases booked £1,000
	£	£	£
Cash at bank and in hand	900 (Dr)	950 (Dr)	50 (Cr)
Sundry debtors	700 (Dr)	700 (Dr)	700 (Dr)
	1,600 (Dr)	1,650 (Dr)	650 (Dr)
Sundry creditors	350 (Cr)	350 (Cr)	350 (Cr)
	1,250 (Dr)	1,300 (Dr)	300 (Dr)

(*c*) If more cash had been received from the debtors, or less cash had been paid to the creditors, or the purchases of £1,000 had been a credit transaction instead of a cash transaction, the closing cash position would have been better although the closing overall monetary position would still have been reduced to £300.

(*d*) As the amount of goods received (purchases) was greater than the amount of goods parted with (sales), the stock of goods unsold at close must have been greater than it was at start. The monetary position could, therefore, be improved by making more sales and reducing stocks held.

EXERCISES

1. Write up the accounts and record the following transactions in the books of A. Cony:

19. .	
Jan. 1	Started with £5,000 in the business bank account.
Jan. 3	Purchased goods on credit terms from R. Supple at a cost of £2,000.
Jan. 5	Bought office furniture for which £250 was paid ex bank on delivery.
Jan. 7	Paid £1,000 on account to R. Supple ex bank.

Carry down the balances in the accounts for cash and R. Supple. Make a complete list of all the balances in the accounts showing that the debits and credits agree.

2. Open the required accounts and write in the entries necessary to record the following transactions in the books of A. Hoot:

19. .	
March 1	Business commenced with £3,000 cash at bank.
March 5	Withdrew £10 from bank for future petty expenditure.
March 7	Made a cash purchase of goods costing £1,000 ex bank.
March 7	Bought stationery costing £2 ex cash in hand.
March 12	Sold goods on credit terms to Q. Kleen for £1,500.
March 13	Made a cash sale of goods for £3 in notes not paid into the bank.
March 14	Paid into the bank £1,000 received from Q. Kleen.

Balance off the accounts and list the balances to show that the accounting equation is satisfied by the records in the books.

3. As at 31 December 19. . the monetary position of a business was as follows:

	£
Cash at bank and in hand	9,222
Sundry debtors	5,146
	14,368
Sundry creditors	7,421
	6,947

(*a*) Compile a statement showing the revised monetary position resulting from the payment into the bank of £2,007 received from a credit client on 1 January 19.1.

(*b*) Show the new monetary position which would result from the payment of £1,596 to a credit supplier 2 January 19.1.

4. The following transactions were completed during the month of June 19. . by the business of L. Middle:

				£
CREDIT SALES OF GOODS: 19..				
	June	3	M. Jonesey	44
	"	5	G. Mixing	120
	"	14	A. Bendy	27
CREDIT PURCHASES OF GOODS:	"	2	J. Fats	163
	"	4	R. Heddy	61
CASH SALES OF GOODS:	"	6	....	10
	"	17	....	35
	"	19	....	6
CASH PURCHASES OF GOODS:	"	15	....	25
	"	30	....	18

The monies received in respect of cash sales and payments of £44 received from M. Jonesey 25 June 19. . and £60 received from G. Mixing 27 June 19. . were paid into the bank. The cash purchases and a payment of £100 to J. Fats 8 June 19. . were made ex bank. The cash at bank 1 June 19. . amounted to £29. Prior to June 19. . all sales and purchases were transacted on a cash basis.

(*a*) Open the relevant accounts, make therein the required double entries and carry down therein the balances at the end of the month.
(*b*) Compile a list of debtors showing the total amount of money owing to the business by the clients as at 30 June 19. .
(*c*) Compile a list of creditors showing the total liability of the business to the suppliers as at 30 June 19. .
(*d*) Compile a statement showing the net overall monetary position of the business as at 30 June 19. .

CHAPTER 4

Recognition of Balances

It will be seen from the explanations already given that many accounts receive entries which are mostly debits OR mostly credits. The Purchases Account receives mainly debits in respect of goods acquired, and the Sales Account mainly credits which represent goods parted with. These accounts may sometimes contain entries of the opposite kind. If a supplier of goods purchased for resale makes an allowance to the business for, say, faulty goods, after the original charge has been recorded as a *debit* in the Purchases Account, a *credit* for the allowance will be entered therein to reduce the amount of the original debit. The difference between the total of the debits and the total of the credits in this account is the cost of the goods acquired for resale (Purchases). This difference is known as 'the balance' in the account. The balance in the Purchases Account will always be a debit balance. Likewise, any allowance made to a client is *debited* to the Sales Account and reduces the total of the *credits* in this account. The balance in the Sales Account will always be a credit balance.

Thus, balances in most accounts can be recognised by their names as being debit balances or credit balances, as the case may be, without this being stated.

Accounts recording costs or expenses will have debit balances.
Accounts recording gains will have credit balances.
Accounts recording fixed assets will have debit balances.

The exceptions to this rule are those accounts which record the type of item which has movements both inwards and outwards which may, on balance, result in either an overall debit balance or an overall credit balance. The main account in this category is the Cash Account (Cash Book) in which monies received and paid into the bank account of the business are recorded as debits and monies paid out of the bank account are recorded as credits. In this case a debit balance is the amount of money which a business has in its bank and a credit balance is the amount by which the business has overdrawn money from its bank. In the Balance Sheet a debit balance in the Cash Account is described as 'Cash at Bank' and a credit balance as 'Bank overdraft'. The former is a current asset and the latter is a current liability.

A balance in the Petty Cash Account must be a debit balance. As one cannot part with loose cash which one does not possess, the credit entries cannot total more than the debit entries. The debit balance is described in the Balance Sheet as 'Cash in hand'. It is a current asset.

Although balances on personal accounts may be either debit or credit balances according to whether they represent money owed to the business or by the business, the clients' accounts and the suppliers' accounts are, as previously stated, grouped into separate ledgers. The clients' accounts in the Sales Ledger will normally show debit balances and the suppliers' accounts in the Purchases Ledger credit balances. The total of all the clients' debit balances in the sales ledger accounts is the total amount of money owed to the business by the clients and is described in the Balance Sheet as 'Sundry debtors'. The total of all the suppliers' credit balances in the purchases ledger accounts is the total amount of money owed by the business to its suppliers and is described in the Balance Sheet as 'Sundry creditors'. 'Sundry debtors' is a CURRENT asset. 'Sundry creditors' is a CURRENT liability.

The student should refer to the list of balances shown on pages 52 and 59 of Chapter 6 and note how they have been collated in the form of a TRIAL BALANCE. He should insert against each balance in this list the type of account which it represents and check the types from the illustrations of the relevant accounts which are also shown in Chapter 6.

When machinery is used, the horizontal form of account is produced. This consists of three columns. The first is for debits (+), the second for credits (−) and a third for balances. A new balance is calculated whenever a new entry is made. This format is illustrated on bank statements. A symbol is shown against each balance to show whether it is debit (+) or credit (−). Mr Bell's cash account for the first week of trading is shown in double-sided form in Chapter 6. In three column horizontal form it would appear as follows:

CASH

Date	Details	Debits	Credits	Balance
1970				
JAN 1	CAPITAL, A. BELL	19,000.00		19,000.00 Dr
JAN 2	RENT		500.00	18,500.00 Dr
JAN 3	OFFICE FIXTURES & FITINGS		300.00	18,200.00 Dr
JAN 3	WAREHOUSE FIXTURES		200.00	18,000.00 Dr
JAN 3	MOTOR DEL. VAN		1,000.00	17,000.00 Dr
JAN 3	STATIONERY		50.00	16,950.00 Dr
JAN 5	PETTY CASH		50.00	16,900.00 Dr
JAN 8	PURCHASES		24,000.00	7,100.00 Cr

This three column format can be used for manual entries but it should be borne in mind that the calculation of a new balance whenever a new entry is made would be time-consuming. Small businesses which have an insignificant number of entries to make generally use the double-sided manual system. Businesses which have a significant number of entries to be made may use a machine, or, if the volume of entries is large enough, a computer.

A computer, suitably programmed and with the proper input, can carry out all the necessary calculations required to print out the Trial Balance from which the Trading and Profit and Loss Account and Balance Sheet are compiled.

Whatever system is used, the importance of being able to identify balances by name and by mathematical status, that is to say whether they be debit (+) or credit (−), cannot be overstated.

EXERCISES

1. From the balances in the books of a merchant, immediately before the revenue accounts were made up, a bookkeeper prepared the incorrect trial balance shown below. It contains no errors in amount, nor have any balances been omitted. It is to be redrafted with the errors corrected and the totals of the debits and credits brought into agreement.

TRIAL BALANCE AS AT 31 DECEMBER 19..

	£	£
Stock, 1 January	1,000	
Cash purchases	959	
Wages	496	
Credit Sales		7,600
Cash sales	26	
Office furniture	470	
Sundry debtors	908	
Telephone expenses		34
Sundry creditors		684
Capital	899	
Rent and rates	242	
Credit purchases		4,291
Cash at bank and in hand	809	
	5,809	12,609

2. The following balances were extracted from the accounts of a retail trader preparatory to making up the Trading and Profit and Loss Account for the year ended 30 June 19.1:

	£
Capital	2,269
Shop fittings	1,750
Delivery vans	2,024
Purchases	7,275
Stationery	51
Rent	700
Cash sales	10,235
Premises	3,000
Cash in hand	223
General expenses	155
Telephones	22
Wages	500
Sundry creditors	1,640
Stock, 1 July 19..	2,010
Postage	24
Bank overdraft	3,218
Credit sales	522
Bank charges	10
Sundry debtors	140

Compile a trial balance from the above figures and state against each balance whether it is real, nominal or personal.

CHAPTER 5

Goods Traded, Stock and Gross Profit

In accounting the possessions of a business are recorded in terms of monetary cost, not as numerical quantities. Each kind of possession (asset) is recorded at cost value in an account. The acquisitions are shown as debits and the disposals as credits *in the same account*. Any allowance made to the business by the supplier of an asset in respect of that asset is recorded as a credit in the account and reduces the cost of the asset. Therefore, the debit balance (debits less credits) in any asset or expense account records the cost value of the particular possession or groups of possessions which the account represents. A debit balance in the Cash Account is the amount of money possessed at the bank. A debit balance in the Motor Delivery Vans Account is the cost value of the motor delivery vans possessed. A debit balance in the Stationery Account is the cost value of the stationery charges held for recovery from clients.

When, however, GOODS held for resale are concerned, acquisitions require debits at COST VALUE but disposals require credits at SELLING VALUE which is considerably higher than cost. Therefore, any balance between THESE debits and credits is meaningless as it does not, in monetary terms, represent the cost of the goods remaining in possession of the business. To calculate this in monetary terms the unit of value must be the same for disposals as for acquisitions.

For example, if a business, having purchased 200 articles at £1 each and sold only 100 of them at £2 each, were to record both of these transactions in one account for goods, in monetary terms the debit entry would be equal to the credit entry and result in a balance of NIL, whereas in fact the business would still have 100 articles in stock unsold:

Dr (+) GOODS Cr (-)

Date	Cash	£200	00	Date	Cash	£200	00

This makes it impossible to record the acquisitions and disposals in the same account. To overcome this difficulty, three accounts instead of one are used for goods traded:

(i) THE PURCHASES ACCOUNT, in which acquisitions (goods purchased for resale) are recorded as debits at cost value, and in which the only credits recorded are for goods returned to suppliers or for any allowances made by the suppliers, which reduce the cost of THE ACQUISITIONS.

(ii) THE SALES ACCOUNT, in which disposals (goods sold) are recorded as credits at selling value, and in which the only debits recorded are for goods returned by the clients or for any allowances made to the clients, which reduce the selling value of THE DISPOSALS.

(iii) THE STOCK ACCOUNT, in which, periodically, at times when the revenue accounts are made up, the cost value of the goods remaining unsold is entered as a debit, the total cost being arrived at by a physical count and calculations at buying prices. This represents the goods possessed by the business and is shown in the Balance Sheet as 'STOCK' under 'Current Assets'.

It should be particularly noted that in accounting, the terms 'PURCHASES' and 'SALES' refer ONLY to acquisitions and disposals of the goods in which a business is trading. These terms must not in any circumstances be related to acquisitions and disposals of fixed assets, nor must fixed assets be considered as or included with 'stock'.

As profit is made from trading in goods at the time when the goods have been sold and delivered to the clients, the GROSS profit must be arrived at by deducting from the total sales value of the goods delivered to clients, the cost of THOSE GOODS ALONE, not the cost of all purchases as shown in the Purchases Account. The latter may be more or less *in quantity* than the goods sold during the trading period. The cost of the goods actually sold and delivered during a trading period is calculated in the Trading Account by adding to the total cost of goods purchased during the trading period, the cost of the stock of goods left over from the previous trading period, and deducting from the resultant figure, the cost of the goods remaining in stock unsold at the end of the present period of trading after all deliveries to clients have been made.

For example, in terms of QUANTITY, if a business commences a trading period with 1,000 articles in stock, adds to this during the trading period purchases of 50,000 articles, and has 16,000 articles remaining in stock after all deliveries to clients have been made at the end of the trading period, it must have disposed of 35,000 articles. In MONETARY terms, the calculation is the same provided each item (stock at start, purchases and stock at close) are expressed at the same cost values. In this example, if each article cost 25p, the cost of the goods sold would be £250, plus £12,500, less £4,000, which equals £8,750. (35,000 articles at 25p each.)

The stock on hand at the close of one trading period becomes the stock at the start of the next trading period. In the first trading period of a newly formed business there cannot, of course, be any stock at the start.

Another difficulty arises as to how the cost value of the goods remaining unsold at the close of each trading period can be inserted into the accounts, when no transaction from which double entries are normally made is entered into. An adjustment has to be made to amend the cost of the purchases acquired during the trading period, to bring it to the cost of the goods sold during the trading period, so that when this is deducted from the SELLING value of the goods sold, the correct amount of gross profit is arrived at in the Trading Account. This is done by making a double entry for bookkeeping purposes which consists of a DEBIT entry in the STOCK ACCOUNT and a CREDIT entry in the TRADING ACCOUNT, for the cost value of the goods remaining unsold. The result of these entries is twofold. When the debit balance in the Purchases Account and the credit balance in the Sales Account have been transferred to the Trading Account, the credit entry for the stock on hand in the Trading Account makes the required correction to the COST of the goods sold during the trading period, and thereby to the resultant gross profit. At the same time, the debit entry in the Stock Account remains therein as a balance which is LISTED in the Balance Sheet as a Current Asset and which will be transferred to the DEBIT of the Trading Account for the following trading period, to serve its purpose as the cost of the goods brought forward for sale in THAT trading period.

A double entry for bookkeeping purposes is also used to transfer an amount from one account to another. To transfer the debit balance in the Purchases Account to the debit of the Trading Account, the Purchases Account is credited and the Trading Account is debited. To transfer the credit balance in the Sales Account to the credit of the Trading Account, the Sales Account is debited and the Trading Account is credited. To transfer the debit in the Stock Account representing the closing stock for the PREVIOUS TRADING PERIOD to the DEBIT of the Trading Account as the stock at the start of the PRESENT PERIOD OF TRADING, the Stock Account is credited and the Trading Account is debited.

Examples of the calculation of the cost of goods sold and the gross profit, together with illustrations of the relevant entries in the Purchases Account, Sales Account, Stock Account and Trading Account, appear on pages 53 and 54 and 60 to 62 in Chapter 6.

In anticipation of a more detailed study of stock control and valuation it should be noted that the market value of goods held in stock, unsold, sometimes drops. Sometimes goods are lost or stolen; sometimes they become unsaleable for one reason or another.

In such cases, if stocks were to be valued at cost and quantities calculated by reference to quantities purchased and sold, the gross and consequently net profits in the revenue accounts would be overstated as would also the asset value in the Stock Account and Balance Sheet.

To overcome this difficulty, only those goods which physically exist as property of the business at the close of a trading period and which are saleable are included in the count and the valuation thereof is taken at their market value when this is lower than cost. This valuation is taken as the figure for stock at close in the Stock Account and the Trading Account, thus automatically reducing the profits calculated in the revenue accounts and the stated value of the asset of stock in the Stock Account and in the Balance Sheet.

In such circumstances the cost of goods sold as calculated in the Trading Account is not in fact the cost of the goods sold alone but the cost of the goods sold plus the additional cost brought about by losses in quantity and/or drop in value of the goods remaining available for sale in the following trading period. This additional cost is automatically taken into account without being shown as a separate item.

Two basic accounting concepts can now be added to those described in the preliminary text which precedes Chapter 1.

MONEY MEASUREMENT. Money as a common measure of value enables different kinds of entities to be added and subtracted. It enables both tangible and intangible things of different natures to be brought together to form joint or composite values. For instance, such things as property, fixtures, machinery and motor vehicles can be added together to form a total value of fixed assets, and costs and expenses can be deducted from gains to form net profit. One cannot, however, add, say, three machines to two vehicles and form a composite entity in terms of quantity, apart, of course, from merely showing that five different items exist, which would be of no value in accounting. This aspect of the Money Measurement Concept may be described as the Concept of Money as a Common Denominator.

One can, of course, add articles of the same kind together to form a meaningful total. The facts recorded in the accounts, however, are shown only in monetary terms; they do not disclose what those facts represent in terms of numerical quantity. This is of particular importance when making comparisons between the results of different periods of trading. Judged in monetary terms, the sales for one period may show a certain percentage of increase or decrease when compared with those for a previous period. Judged in numerical terms of quantity, this percentage of increase or decrease may be proven false because a rise or fall in price has increased or decreased the monetary value per article. For instance, in a business which has sold, in one period, 100 articles at £1 each (£100) and has sold, in the following period, 100 of the same kind of article at £1.20 each (£120), the sales in monetary terms will show an increase of 20% (£20) whereas, in fact, there has been no real increase in numerical terms.

This disadvantage also applies to costs and expenses which rise or fall in monetary value with changes in the value of the pound. Inflation will tend to increase, and deflation tend to decrease, the prices of all goods and services. The quantities of goods purchased and sold, and expenses such as stationery used, cannot be measured in monetary terms unless prices remain stable. The increases or decreases in gains, costs and expenses, when prices are fluctuating, can be measured in monetary terms only approximately and only in relation to each other. This aspect of the Money Measurement Concept may be described as the Concept of the Stability of Currency.

Another aspect of the Money Measurement Concept is the limitation which the recording of business transactions in monetary terms places upon the amount of information relevant to management which can be extracted from the accounts. Matters such as the quality of management, the position held in a market by the products of a business, the state of the competition, whether or not there is likely to be a shortage of supplies, or the relationship which exists between management and factory personnel, are not disclosed by the monetary information recorded in the accounts.

Although sound assessment of what information in monetary terms is useful to management and suitable analysis and interpretation of such information is of great value to management, there must always be an awareness that much other information which cannot be recorded in monetary terms is essential to efficient management. Whenever interpretation of accounting information is undertaken, consideration must be given to all factors outside those recorded in the accounts which may affect the validity of the conclusions to which the interpretation, in monetary terms alone, points.

REALISATION. The Realisation Concept lays down the principle that the point in time at which a profit or loss is realised is when the goods or services sold are delivered. For accounting purposes a profit or loss is made at the time when the purchaser of goods or services traded becomes legally liable to pay for them, irrespective of the date on which the contract of sale was established and irrespective of the date on which payment was made. Two or three of these events may, of course, coincide, as they do when payment is made at the time of delivery or when cash sales are made in retail businesses.

The fact alone of a contract of sale having been made does not permit its value to be included in the accounts. The fact of payment not having been made for goods or services sold and delivered does not permit the exclusion of their sales value from the accounts. The date against which the monetary value of a sale is recorded in the accounts must be the date on which despatch or delivery of the goods or services sold is made to the client, so that the profit or loss contained in the sale is taken into account in the correct trading period, according to the Realisation Concept.

The concept is not a perfect one as the profit taken into one period may have to be taken out of a later period as a result of some unforeseen event, such as the return of faulty goods from a client at some time after the accounts in which the sale was included, have been finalised. If, however, at the time of finalising the accounts for a period of trading, it is known that an allowance will be made later, an adjustment should be made in the accounts to provide for it.

If a future allowance to a client is merely a possibility, a judgement has to be exercised as to whether the amount envisaged is of sufficient consequence in the calculation of profit or loss to warrant mention of it in the accounts as a contingency.

Recognition of the necessity for making judgements as to what is of consequence to the validity of the statements made in the Profit and Loss Account and Balance Sheet of a business, when deciding how certain items are to be recorded in the accounts, has led to the concept of materiality which is dealt with at a later stage in the study of accounting.

EXERCISES

1. Explain the two aspects of the Money Measurement Concept giving your suggestions as to matters concerning which the figures recorded in a set of accounts give no information or, if taken on their face value, may give a false impression.
2. Describe the principles contained in the Realisation Concept.
3. A newly formed business purchased for cash 1,000 articles at £2 each on 1st January 19. . and on 31st January 19. . sold for cash 500 of the articles at £3 each. Show the entries in the Purchases, Sales, Stock and Trading Accounts and carry down the gross profit in the Trading Account for the month ended 31st January 19. .
4. A firm commenced on 1st April 19. . with 500 articles in stock which had been purchased at 30 pence each. During the following twelve months it purchased 3,000 articles at 25 pence each. During the same period it sold, at 40 pence each, 400 articles which had cost 30 pence each and, at 35 pence each, 2,000 articles which had cost 25 pence each.

   (*a*) Show your calculation of the cost value of the stock on hand as at 31st March 19.1.

   (*b*) Compile, in traditional form, the Trading Account for the year ended 31st March 19.1.

   (*c*) Show the relevant entries in the Stock Account.

5. Open the appropriate accounts and record the following transactions:

19. .	
Oct. 1	J. Kayne started a business with £10,000 cash at bank.
Oct. 3	Paid, ex bank, £60 rent for the month of October.
Oct. 5	Purchased office furniture and fittings at a cost of £700 ex bank.
Oct. 6	Purchased on credit terms from L. Pony goods costing £6,000.
Oct. 8	Sold goods for £2,300 for which a cheque was received at the time of delivery.
Oct. 12	Made a cash purchase of goods in exchange for a cheque amounting to £12,250.
Oct. 24	Gave credit to S. Teeman for goods sold for £9,100.
Oct. 25	Bought a motor van for £800 ex bank.
Oct. 25	Withdrew from bank £20 for petty expenditure.
Oct. 31	Paid £18 ex cash in hand in settlement of general expenses.

Compile the Trial Balance as at 31st October 19. .
Make the entries necessary to complete the Trading Account and carry down therein the gross profit for the month. The stock at 31st October 19. . was valued at £11,341. The Profit and Loss Account is not required.

6. The trial balance following was extracted from the books of L. Sooper as at 31st December 19.1:

TRIAL BALANCE 31 DECEMBER 19.1

	£	£
Stock 1 January 19.1	1,000	
Cash Purchases	950	
Credit purchases	4,241	
Wages	439	
Credit sales		6,205
Cash sales		605
Furniture and fittings	470	
Sundry debtors and creditors	910	680
Postage and stationery	32	
Rent and rates	248	
Capital, L. Sooper 1 January 19.1		800
	8,290	8,290

The stock on hand was valued, on 31st December 19.1 at £921.
L. Sooper commenced business 1 January 19. . with capital of £1,000.

(*a*) Prepare, in vertical form, the Trading section of the revenue accounts for the year ended 31 December 19.1.
(*b*) Show your calculation of the net profit or loss for the year ended 31st December 19. .
(The Profit and Loss section of the revenue accounts is not required.)

Practice and Illustration

In order to illustrate the principles described in the preceding text and to provide practical examples for reference when studying the text, the following takes the student, step by step, through a limited number of basic transactions involved in the first two yearly periods of trading carried out by the merchant business of a sole trader. It will be realised that, in practice, the number of transactions entered into by such a business would be far in excess of those used in these examples, particularly as regards purchases and sales of goods traded and the number of personal accounts of suppliers and clients which would be required therefor. The number of different kinds of expenses would also be greater.

1*st January*, 1970

Mr A. Bell paid £19,000 into the bank account opened for the business, to enable trading to commence.

			CAPITAL A.BELL			(Personal)			A/C ref: GL/1		
						1970					
						Jan	1	Cash	CB/1	19,000	-

			CASH BOOK			(Real)			A/C ref: CB/1		
1970											
Jan	1	Capital, A.Bell	GL/1	19,000	-						

2*nd January*, 1970

Rent for the year to 31st December, 1970 was paid by cheque to the owner of the premises occupied by the business – £500.

			RENT PAYABLE			(Nominal)			A/C ref: NL/1		
1970											
Jan	2	Cash	CB/1	500	-						

			CASH BOOK			(Real)			A/C ref: CB/1		
1970						1970					
JAN	1	CAPITAL, A.BELL	GL/1	19,000	-	Jan	2	Rent	NL/1	500	-

Each account is identified by its name and reference. The two opposite entries required for every transaction are cross-referenced in their respective accounts. In each account its type is indicated in brackets. The letters used in the account references are abbreviations for Cash Book (CB), Petty Cash Book (PC), Sales Ledger (SL), Purchases Ledger (PL), Nominal Ledger (NL), and General Ledger (GL). In this case a General Ledger has been used to contain the Capital Account, the accounts for fixed assets, the Stock Account and the Revenue Accounts. In order to illustrate the changes which take place in the accounts as each new transaction, or group of transactions is recorded, the relevant accounts are re-illustrated complete with the previous entries made therein, shown in capitals, the new entries being shown in lower case.

3rd January, 1970

Paid by cheques for office fixtures and fittings £300, warehouse fixtures £200, a motor van for deliveries to clients £1,000, and stationery (letter headings, invoice forms, etc.) £50.

OFFICE FIXTURES & FITTINGS (Real)									A/C ref: GL/2	
1970 Jan	3	Cash	CB/1	300	-					

WAREHOUSE FIXTURES (Real)									A/C ref: GL/3	
1970 Jan	3	Cash	CB/1	200	-					

MOTOR DELIVERY VANS (Real)									A/C ref: GL/4	
1970 Jan	3	Cash	CB/1	1,000	-					

STATIONERY (Nominal)									A/C ref: NL/2	
1970 Jan	3	Cash	CB/1	50	-					

CASH BOOK (Real)									A/C ref: CB/1	
1970 JAN	1	CAPITAL, A. BELL	GL/1	19,000	-	1970 JAN	2	RENT	NL/1	500	-
						"	3	Office Fixtures & Fittings	GL/2	300	-
						"	"	Warehouse Fixtures	GL/3	200	-
						"	"	Motor Delivery Van	GL/4	1,000	-
						"	"	Stationery	NL/2	50	-

5th January, 1970

Withdrew by cheque from the bank for small sundry items of expenditure, the sum of £50 in notes and coin.

PETTY CASH BOOK (Real) — A/C ref: PC/1

1970 Jan	5	Cash	CB/1	50	-						

CASH BOOK (Real) — A/C ref: CB/1

1970 JAN	1	CAPITAL, A.BELL	GL/1	19,000	-	1970 JAN	2	RENT	NL/1	500	-
						"	3	OFFICE FIX/FTTNGS	GL/2	300	-
						"	"	WAREHOUSE FIXTURES	GL/3	200	-
						"	"	MOTOR DELIVERY VAN	GL/4	1,000	-
						"	"	STATIONERY	NL/2	50	-
						"	5	Petty Cash	PC/1	50	-

6th January, 1970

Expended petty cash, on Postage Stamps £22, and on sundry expenses £18.

POSTAGE (Nominal) — A/C ref: NL/3

1970 Jan	6	Petty Cash	PC/1	22	-						

SUNDRY EXPENSES (Nominal) — A/C ref: NL/4

1970 Jan	6	Petty Cash	PC/1	18	-						

PETTY CASH BOOK (Real) — A/C ref: PC/1

1970 JAN	5	CASH	CB/1	50	-	1970 Jan	6	Postage	NL/3	22	-
						"	"	Sundry expenses	NL/4	18	-

8th January, 1970

A stock of goods for resale was purchased, involving two transactions, one being a cash transaction and the other a credit transaction.

A cheque was drawn and paid immediately for goods costing £24,000 from one supplier. The remainder of the goods costing £11,000 were purchased on credit terms from another supplier, G. Greening Ltd, with a promise to pay for them by the end of January 1971. The bank had agreed to a temporary overdraft up to a limit of £8,000 to enable the cash transaction to be made.

PURCHASES (Nominal) A/C ref: NL/5

1970										
Jan	8	Cash	CB/1	24,000 -						
"	"	G.Greening Ltd	PL/1	11,000 -						

CASH BOOK (Real) A/C ref: CB/1

1970					1970				
JAN	1	CAPITAL, A.BELL	GL/1	19,000 -	JAN	2	RENT	NL/1	500 -
"	8	Balance c/down	c/d	7,100 -	"	3	OFFICE FIX/FITTGS	GL/2	300 -
					"	"	WAREHOUSE FIXTURES	GL/3	200 -
					"	"	MOTOR DELIVERY VAN	GL/4	1,000 -
					"	"	STATIONERY	NL/2	50 -
					"	5	PETTY CASH	PC/1	50 -
					"	8	Purchases	NL/5	24,000 -
				26,100 -					26,100 -
					Jan	9	Balance (Overdraft) brought down	b/d	7,100 -

Note how the excess of the total of the credit entries over the total of the debit entries, forms a credit balance, and how this credit balance is carried down and brought down into the credit side of the account.

G. Greening Ltd., (Personal) A/C ref: PL/1
14 Long Square,
Birmingham.

					1970				
					Jan	8	Purchases	NL/5	11,000 -

24th January, 1970

Goods were sold and delivered to three clients as follows:

(i) A cash sale to J. Smithby who took goods for which a charge of £56 was made, and for which he paid on delivery in notes. This money was paid into the bank.

(ii) A cash sale to M. Saxy & Company for goods to the value of £84 for which payment was made on delivery by cheque. This cheque was also paid into the bank.

(iii) A credit sale to Whitson Ltd. of goods invoiced at £21,000, payment for which was to be made in two amounts, £10,000 by the last day of January, 1970 and £11,000 by the 31st March 1970.

SALES (Nominal) A/C ref: NL/6

						1970					
						Jan	24	Cash	CB/1	56	-
						"	"	Cash	CB/1	84	-
						"	"	Witson Ltd.	SL/1	21,000	

CASH BOOK (real) A/C ref: CB/1

1970						1970					
Jan	24	Sales	NL/6	56	-	JAN	9	BALANCE			
"	"	Sales	NL/6	84	-			(OVERDRAFT)	B/D	7,100	-

Witson Ltd., (Personal) A/C ref: SL/1
2 Market Square,
London,. EC2

1970											
Jan	24	Sales	NL/6	21,000	-						

28th January, 1970

A cheque for £10,000 was received from Whitson Ltd. and paid into the bank.

CASH BOOK (real) A/C ref: CB/1

1970						1970					
Jan	24	SALES	NL/6	56	-	JAN	9	BALANCE			
"	"	SALES	NL/6	84	-			(OVERDRAFT)	B/D	7,100	-
"	28	Whitson Ltd.	SL/6	10,000	-						

Witson Ltd., (Personal) A/C ref: SL/1
2 Market Square,
London, EC2

1970						1970					
Jan	24	SALES	NL/6	21,000	-	Jan	28	Cash	CB/1	10,000	-
						"	28	Balance	c/d	11,000	-
				21,000	-			carried down		21,000	-
Jan	29	Balance brought down	b/d	11,000	-						

Note here how the balance on the account, in this case a debit balance, is carried down and brought down into the debit side.

31*st January*, 1970

Salaries for the month amounted to £494. This amount was withdrawn by cheque from the bank in notes and paid to the employees.

SALARIES (Nominal) A/C ref: NL/7

1970										
Jan	31	Cash	CB/1	494 -						

CASH BOOK (real) A/C ref: CB/1

1970					1970					
Jan	24	SALES	NL/6	56 -	JAN	9	BALANCE			
"	"	SALES	NL/6	84 -			(OVERDRAFT)	B/D	7,100	-
"	28	WHITSON LTD.	SL/1	10 ,000 -	"	31	Salaries	NL/7	494	-

28*th February*, 1970

Paid salaries for the month £524.

SALARIES (Nominal) A/C ref: NL/7

1970										
JAN	31	CASH	CB/1	494 -						
Feb	28	Cash	CB/1	524 -						

CASH BOOK (real) A/C ref: CB/1

1970					1970					
Jan	24	SALES	NL/6	56 -	JAN	9	BALANCE			
"	"	SALES	NL/6	84 -			(OVERDRAFT)	B/D	7,100	-
"	28	WHITSON LTD.	SL/1	10,000 -	"	31	SALARIES	NL/7	494	-
					Feb	28	Salaries	NL/7	524	

31*st March*, 1970

Paid salaries for the month £524.
Paid into the bank a cheque for £11,000 received from Whitson Ltd.
Paid by cheque, the telephone charges for the Quarter £20.

CASH BOOK (real) A/C ref: CB/1

1970					1970					
Jan	24	SALES	NL/6	56 -	JAN	9	BALANCE			
"	"	SALES	NL/6	84 -			(OVERDRAFT)	B/D	7,100	-
"	28	WHITSON LTD.	SL/1	10,000 -	"	31	SALARIES	NL/7	494	-
Mar	31	Whitson Ltd.	SL/1	11,000 -	FEB	28	SALARIES	NL/7	524	-
					Mar	31	Salaries	NL/7	524	-
					"	"	Telephones	NL/8	20	-

SALARIES (Nominal)										A/C ref: NL/7	
1970											
JAN	31	CASH	CB/1	494	-						
FEB	28	CASH	CB/1	524	-						
MAR	31	Cash	CB/1	524	-						

Whitson Ltd. (Personal)										A/C ref: SL/1	
2 Market Square											
London, EC2											
1970						1970					
Jan	29	BALANCE b/d	b/d	11,000	-	Mar	31	Cash	CB/1	11,000	-

TELEPHONES (Nominal)										A/C ref: NL/8	
1970											
Mar	31	Cash	CB/1	20	-						

6th April 1970

Sold goods on credit terms to J. Baking & Company £2,050.

10th April 1970

Sold goods on credit terms to C. Elling Ltd. £950.

21st April 1970

Sold goods on credit terms to C. Elling Ltd. £1,000.

SALES (Nominal)										A/C ref: NL/6	
						1970					
						JAN	24	CASH	CB/1	56	-
						"	"	CASH	CB/1	84	-
						"	"	WHITSON LTD.	SL/1	21,000	-
						Apl.	6	J.Baking & Co.	SL/2	2,050	-
						"	10	C.Elling Ltd.	SL/3	950	-
						"	21	C.Elling Ltd.	SL/3	1,000	-

J. Baking & Company (Personal)										A/C ref: SL/2	
12 Bank Row,											
Bedford.											
1970											
Apl	6	Sales	NL/6	2,050	-						

C. Elling Ltd., (Personal)										A/C ref: SL/3	
51 Older Road,											
Dunstable.											
1970											
Apl	10	Sales	NL/6	950	-						
"	21	Sales	NL/6	1,000	-						

30th April 1970
Paid the salaries for the month - £524.

14th May 1970
Sold goods on credit terms to H. Greenacre Ltd. for £10,000 in respect of which two payments were to be made, one of £5,000 by the end of September 1970 and the other of £5,000 by the end of January 1971.

30th May 1970
Paid the salaries for the month £524.
Received a cheque for £500 from J. Baking and Company being part payment for goods delivered on the 6th April 1970 and a cheque for £950 from C. Elling Ltd. in payment for goods delivered on 10th April 1970.
Both cheques were paid into the bank account of the business.

30th June 1970
Paid the salaries for the month - £524.
Sent a cheque to the Post Office in settlement of the telepho charges for the quarter - £30.

31st July 1970
Paid the salaries for the month - £524.

31st August 1970
Paid the salaries for the month - £524.

30th September 1970
Paid the salaries for the month - £524.
Paid telephone charges by cheque £32.
Paid into the bank a cheque received from C. Elling Ltd - £50

31st October 1970
Paid the salaries for the month - £524.
Received and paid into the bank a cheque for £5,000 from H. Greenacre Ltd.

17th November 1970
Received a cheque for £550 from J.Baking & Company and paid it into the bank.

24th November 1970
Paid to G. Greening Ltd. by cheque £5,000 in part payment for the goods purchased from them on 8th January 1970.

25th November 1970
Purchased goods on credit terms for £14,100 from C.Mending & Co. Ltd.

30th November 1970
Paid the salaries for the month - £524.

6th December 1970
Sold goods on credit terms to S. Milkin Ltd. for £14,400
Sold goods for £500 to a client who paid by cheque upon delivery.
Obtained from C. Mending & Co.Ltd. a credit note for faulty goods - £100.

28th December 1970
Paid into bank a cheque for £13,860 received from S. Milkin Ltd.
Sent a credit note to S. Milkin Ltd for goods short-delivered £40.

31st December 1970
Paid the salaries for the month - £524.
Paid telephone charges by cheque £40.
It was found the bank had charged the businesswith £1 for a service rendered, and £29 for interest on the overdraft which existed for a time during January 1970.
With a view to expanding the business during 1971 the followi fixed assets were acquired by cash transactions, payments bei made by cheques - Premises £15,000, Plant & Machinery £4,000, Warehouse Fixtures £1,500, and Motor Delivery Van £1,000.
Paid £2,000 by cheque to C. Mending & Co.Ltd.

		SALARIES (Nominal)							A/C ref: NL/7		
1970											
JAN	31	CASH	CB/1	494	-						
FEB	28	CASH	CB/1	524	-						
MAR	31	CASH	CB/1	524	-						
APL	30	Cash	CB/1	524	-						
May	30	Cash	CB/1	524	-						
June	30	Cash	CB/1	524	-						
July	31	Cash	CB/1	524	-						
Aug	31	Cash	CB/1	524	-						
Sept	30	Cash	CB/1	524	-						
Oct	31	Cash	CB/1	524	-						
Nov	30	Cash	CB/1	524	-						
Dec	31	Cash	CB/1	524	-						

		CASH BOOK (Real)							A/C ref: CB/1		
1970						1970					
JAN	24	SALES	NL/6	56	-	JAN	9	BALANCE	B/d	7,100	-
"	24	SALES	NL/6	84	-	"	31	SALARIES	NL/7	494	-
"	28	WHITSON LTD.	SL/1	10,000	-	FEB	28	SALARIES	NL/7	524	-
MAR	31	WHITSON LTD.	SL/1	11,000	-	MAR	31	SALARIES	NL/7	524	-
May	30	J.Baking &Co.	SL/2	500	-	"	"	TELEPHONES	NL/8	20	-
"	"	C.Elling Ltd.	SL/3	950	-	APL	30	Salaries	NL/7	524	-
Sept	30	C.Elling Ltd.	SL/3	500	-	May	30	Salaries	NL/7	524	-
Oct	31	H.Greenacre	SL/4	5,000	-	June	30	Salaries	NL/7	524	-
Nov	17	J.Baking &Co.	SL/2	550	-	"	"	Telephones	NL/8	30	-
Dec	6	Sales	NL/6	500	-	July	31	Salaries	NL/7	524	-
"	28	S.Milkin Ltd.	SL/5	13,860	-	Aug	31	Salaries	NL/7	524	-
						Sept	30	Salaries	NL/7	524	-
						"	"	Telephones	NL/8	32	-
						Oct	31	Salaries	NL/7	524	-
						Nov	24	G.Greening Ltd	PL/1	5,000	-
						"	30	Salaries	NL/7	524	-
						Dec	31	Salaries	NL/7	524	-
						"	"	Telephones	NL/8	40	-
						"	"	Bank Chg & Int	NL/9	30	-
						"	"	Premises	GL/5	15,000	-
						"	"	Plant & Mach	GL/6	4,000	-
						"	"	Warehouse Fix	GL/3	1,500	-
						"	"	Motor Del Van	GL/4	1,000	-
						"	"	C.Mending & Co	PL/2	2,000	-
						"	"	Balance	c/d	990	-
				43,000	-					43,000	-
1971											
Jan	1	Balance	b/d	990	-						

		H. Greenacre Ltd. (Personal)							A/C ref: SL/4		
		4 Main Street,									
		Elstree.									
1970						1970					
May	14	Sales	NL/6	10,000	-	Oct	31	Cash	CB/1	5,000	-

SALES (Nominal)											A/C ref: NL/6	
1970						1970						
Dec	28	S.Milkin Ltd.	SL/5	40	-	JAN	24	CASH	CB/1	56	-	
						"	"	CASH	CB/1	84	-	
						"	"	WHITSON LTD.	SL/1	21,000	-	
						APL	6	J.BAKING & CO	SL/2	2,050	-	
						"	10	C.ELLING LTD.	SL/3	950	-	
						"	21	C.ELLING LTD.	SL/3	1,000	-	
						May	14	H.Greenacre Ltd	SL/4	10,000	-	
						Dec	6	S.Milkin Ltd.	SL/5	14,400	-	
						"	6	Cash	CB/1	500	-	

J. Baking & Company (Personal)											A/C ref: SL/2
12 Bank Row,											
Bedford.											
1970						1970					
APL	6	SALES	NL/6	2,050	-	May	30	Cash	CB/1	500	-
						Sept	17	Cash	CB/1	550	-

C. Elling Ltd. (Personal)											A/C ref: SL/3
51 Older Road,											
Dunstable.											
1970						1970					
APL	10	SALES	NL/6	950	-	May	30	Cash	CB/1	950	-
"	21	SALES	NL/6	1,000	-	Sept	30	Cash	CB/1	500	-

TELEPHONES (Nominal)											A/C ref: NL/8
1970											
MAR	31	CASH	CB/1	20	-						
June	30	Cash	CB/1	30	-						
Sept	30	Cash	CB/1	32	-						
Dec	31	Cash	CB/1	40	-						

G. Greening Ltd. (Personal)											A/C ref: PL/1
14 Long Square,											
Birmingham.											
1970						1970					
Nov	24	Cash	CB/1	5,000	-	JAN	8	PURCHASES	NL/5	11,000	-

All the transactions entered into during the year 1970 by Mr A. Bell's business having been recorded in the accounts, it was now necessary to make up the Trading Account to ascertain the gross profit, and the Profit and Loss Account to ascertain the net profit. To organise this work efficiently, a list of the balances outstanding in the accounts was compiled, as a working reference and to make sure that the total of the debits or debit balances was equal to the total of the credits or credit balances. This list is called a TRIAL BALANCE. It can be made up in traditional form as shown in the first of the following extractions or in vertical form as shown in the second. Note that a trial balance is NOT AN ACCOUNT, but a list of the balances in the accounts

C. Mending & Co. Ltd. (Personal)										A/C ref:	PL/2
8 Winding Lane, Bristol											
1970						1970					
Dec	6	Purc. (faulty goods)	NL/5	100	-	Nov	25	Purchases	NL/5	14,100	-
"	31	Cash	CB/1	2,000	-						

PURCHASES (Nominal)										A/C ref:	NL/5
1970						1970					
JAN	8	CASH	CB/1	24,000	-	Dec	6	C. Mending & Co. Ltd.	PL/2	100	-
JAN	8	G.GREENING LTD.	PL/1	11,000	-						
Nov	24	C.Mending & Co. Ltd.	PL/2	14,100	-						

S. Milkin Ltd. (Personal)										A/C ref:	SL/5
19 Rolling Avenue, Greenford.											
1970						1970					
Dec	6	Sales	NL/6	14,400	-	Dec	28	Cash	CB/1	13,860	-
						"	"	Sales (Short Del)	NL/6	40	-

BANK CHARGES AND INTEREST (NOMINAL)										A/C ref:	NL/9
1970											
Dec	31	Cash	CB/1	30	-						

PREMISES (real)										A/C ref:	GL/5
1970											
Dec	31	Cash	CB/1	15,000	-						

PLANT & MACHINERY (real)										A/C ref:	GL/6
1970											
Dec	31	Cash	CB/1	4,000	-						

WAREHOUSE FIXTURES (real)										A/C ref:	GL/3
1970											
JAN	3	CASH	CB/1	200	-						
Dec	31	Cash	CB/1	1,500	-						

MOTOR DELIVERY VANS (real)										A/C ref:	GL/4
1970											
JAN	3	CASH	CB/1	1,000	-						
Dec	31	Cash	CB/1	1,000	-						

before the revenue accounts are compiled. The account references are sometimes shown so that the accounts may easily be found in the ledgers.

It should be noted that in a trial balance, provided there are no errors in arriving at the balances in the accounts, when all positive (debit) balances and all negative (credit) balances are totalled independently, their respective totals are equal; also, that when both positive (debit) balances and negative (credit) balances are totalled together in one list they cancel each other out and the overall total is NIL.

TRIAL BALANCE AS AT 31st DECEMBER 1970		A/C Ref.	DEBITS		CREDITS	
			£		£	
Motor Delivery Vans		GL/4	2,000	-		
Warehouse Fixtures		GL/3	1,700	-		
Plant & Machinery		GL/6	4,000	-		
Premises		GL/5	15,000	-		
Bank Charges and Interest		NL/9	30	-		
Sundry Debtors:	S.Milkin Ltd	SL/5	500	-		
	C.Elling Ltd	SL/3	500	-		
	J.Baking & Company	SL/2	1,000	-		
	H.Greenacre Ltd	SL/4	5,000	-		
Purchases		NL/5	49,000	-		
Sundry Creditors:	C.Mending & Co.Ltd	PL/2			12,000	-
	G.Greening Ltd	PL/1			6,000	-
Telephones		NL/8	122	-		
Sales		NL/6			50,000	-
Cash at Bank		CB/1	990	-		
Salaries		NL/7	6,258	-		
Cash in Hand		PC/1	10	-		
Sundry Expenses		NL/4	18	-		
Postage		NL/3	22	-		
Stationery		NL/2	50	-		
Office Fixtures & Fittings		GL/2	300	-		
Rent Payable		NL/1	500	-		
Capital, A. Bell		GL/1			19,000	-
			87,000	-	87,000	-

TRIAL BALANCE AS AT 31ST DECEMBER 1970

Motor Delivery Vans	2,000 -	+
Warehouse Fixtures	1,700 -	+
Plant & Machinery	4,000 -	+
Premises	15,000 -	+
Bank Charges & Interest	30 -	+
S. Milkin Ltd.	500 -	+
C. Elling Ltd.	500 -	+
J. Baking & Company	1,000 -	+
H. Greenacre Ltd.	5,000 -	+
Purchases	49,000 -	+
C. Mending & Co. Ltd.	12,000 -	-
G. Greening Ltd.	6,000 -	-
Telephones	122 -	+
Sales	50,000 -	-
Cash at Bank	990 -	+
Salaries	6,258 -	+
Cash in hand	10 -	+
Sundry Expenses	18 -	+
Postage	22 -	+
Stationery	50 -	+
Office Fixutres & Fittings	300 -	+
Rent payable	500 -	+
Capital, A. Bell	19,000 -	-
	NIL	

Using this list as a guide the Revenue Acccunts were made up. The stock of goods on hand at the 31st December, 1970 was counted and valued at £11,000, at cost.

Firstly the Trading Account was made up to ascertain the gross profit for the Year.

It can be seen that the figures in the Trading and Profit & Loss Accounts represent totals for the trading period, not transactions which have taken place on specific dates. Consequently, each of these revenue accounts is headed to show clearly the period which it covers, and the date columns therein are left blank.

SALES (Nominal) A/C Ref: NL/6

1970						1970					
DEC	28	S.MILKIN LTD	SL/5	40	-	JAN	24	CASH	CB/1	56	-
"	31	Bal. to Trading A/C	GL/8	50,000	-	"	"	CASH	CB/1	84	-
						"	"	WHITSON LTD	SL/1	21,000	-
						APR	6	J.BAKING & CO	SL/2	2,050	-
						"	10	C.ELLING LTD	SL/3	950	-
						"	21	C.ELLING LTD	SL/3	1,000	-
						MAY	14	H.GREENACRE LTD	SL/4	10,000	-
						DEC	6	S.MILKIN LTD	SL/5	14,400	-
						"	"	CASH	CB/1	500	-
				50,040	-					50,040	-

PURCHASES (Nominal) A/C Ref: NL/5

1970						1970					
JAN	8	CASH	CB/1	24,000	-	DEC	6	C.MENDING & CO LTD	PL/2	100	-
"	"	G.GREENING LTD	PL/1	11,000	-	"	31	Bal to Trading A/C	GL/8	49,000	-
NOV	24	C.MENDING & CO. LTD	PL/2	14,100	-						
				49,100	-					49,100	-

STOCK (Real) A/C Ref: GL/7

1970											
Dec	31	Trading Account	GL/8	11,000	-						

TRADING ACCOUNT FOR THE YEAR ENDED 31st DECEMBER 1970 (REVENUE) A/C Ref: GL/8

		Purchases	NL/5	49,000	-			Sales	NL/6	50,000	-
		Gross Profit to Profit & Loss A/C	GL/9	12,000	-			Stock in hand at close	GL/7	11,000	-
				61,000	-					61,000	-

PROFIT & LOSS ACCOUNT FOR THE YEAR ENDED 31st DECEMBER 1970 (REVENUE) A/C Ref: GL/9

								Gross Profit from Trading A/C	GL/8	12,000	-

It can also be seen that the transfers of the balances from the sales and purchases accounts cancel the figures therein and leave these nominal accounts cleared to receive entries in respect of new transactions during the next period of trading, whereas the balance in the Stock Account remains outstanding in this real account representing goods in possession of the business at the end of this first period of trading. It will be listed in the Balance Sheet as a current asset.

In vertical form the Trading Account would appear as follows:

Trading Account for the
year ended 31st December 1970

	£				£
Sales	50,000 -		Sales		50,000 -
Stock at close	11,000 -		Purchases	49,000 +	
	61,000 -	OR	Stock at close	11,000 -	
Purchases	49,000 +		Cost of goods sold		38,000 +
Gross Profit	12,000 -		Gross profit		12,000 -

Although it is not the usual practice, the balances left in the accounts after the sales and purchases accounts have been cleared, are listed below. This list illustrates the position in the accounts after the Trading Account has been made up and before the Profit and Loss Account has been compiled. It also shows that the balances used in the Trading Account have been eliminated from their nominal accounts and new balances, one in the Trading Account (gross profit) and another in the Stock Account (goods for resale held in possession of the business), have been created.

	£	DEBITS £	CREDITS £
Motor Delivery Vans	2,000 +	2,000	
Warehouse Fixtures	1,700 +	1,700	
Plant and Machinery	4,000 +	4,000	
Premises	15,000 +	15,000	
Bank charges & interest	30 +	30	
S.Milkin Ltd	500 +	500	
C.Elling Ltd	500 +	500	
J.Baking & Company	1,000 +	1,000	
H.Greenacre Ltd	5,000 +	5,000	
C.Mending & Co.Ltd	12,000 -		12,000
G.Greening Ltd	6,000 -		6,000
Telephones	122 +	122	
Cash at bank	990 +	990	
Salaries	6,258 +	6,258	
Cash in hand	10 +	10	
Sundry expenses	18 +	18	
Postage	22 +	22	
Stationery	50 +	50	
Office Furniture & Fittings	300 +	300	
Rents payable	500 +	500	
Capital A. Bell	19,000 -		19,000
Gross profit	12,000 -		12,000
Stock at close	11,000 +	11,000	
	NIL	49,000	49,000

After the Trading Account had been prepared, the Profit and Loss Account was made up to ascertain the net profit for the year.

SALARIES (Nominal) A/C ref: NL/7

1970						1970					
JAN	31	CASH	CB/1	494	-	DEC	31	Balance to Profit & Loss Account	GL/9	6,258	-
FEB	28	CASH	CB/1	524	-						
MAR	31	CASH	CB/1	524	-						
APL	30	CASH	CB/1	524	-						
MAY	30	CASH	CB/1	524	-						
JUNE	30	CASH	CB/1	524	-						
JULY	31	CASH	CB/1	524	-						
AUG	31	CASH	CB/1	524	-						
SEPT	30	CASH	CB/1	524	-						
OCT	31	CASH	CB/1	524	-						
NOV	30	CASH	CB/1	524	-						
DEC	31	CASH	CB/1	524	-						
				6,258	-					6,258	-

RENT PAYABLE (Nominal) A/C ref: NL/1

1970						1970					
JAN	2	CASH	CB/1	500	-	Dec	31	Balance to Profit & Loss Account	GL/9	500	-

TELEPHONES (Nominal) A/C ref: NL/8

1970						1970					
MAR	31	CASH	CB/1	20	-	Dec	31	Balance to Profit & Loss Account	GL/9	122	-
JUNE	30	CASH	CB/1	30	-						
SEPT	30	CASH	CB/1	32	-						
DEC	31	CASH	CB/1	40	-						
				122	-					122	-

STATIONERY (Nominal) A/C ref: NL/2

1970						1970					
JAN	3	CASH	CB/1	50	-	Dec	31	Balance to Profit & Loss Account	GL/9	50	-

POSTAGE (Nominal) A/C ref: NL/3

1970						1970					
JAN	6	PETTY CASH	PC/1	22	-	Dec	31	Balance to Profit & Loss Account	GL/9	22	-

SUNDRY EXPENSES (Nominal) A/C ref: NL/4

1970						1970					
JAN	6	PETTY CASH	PC/1	18	-	Dec	31	Balance to Profit & Loss Account	GL/9	18	-

BANK CHARGES & INTEREST (Nominal)									A/C ref: NL/9
1970 DEC	31	CASH	CB/1	30 -	1970 Dec	31	Balance to Profit and Loss Account	GL/9	30 -

PROFIT & LOSS ACCOUNT FOR THE YEAR ENDED 31ST DECEMBER, 1970									A/C ref: GL/9
		Salaries	NL/7	6,258 -			GROSS PROFIT FROM TRADING ACCOUNT	GL/8	12,000 -
		Rent	NL/1	500 -					
		Telephones	NL/8	122 -					
		Stationery	NL/2	50 -					
		Postage	NL/3	22 -					
		Sundry Expns.	NL/4	18 -					
		Bank Charges & Interest	NL/9	30 -					
		Net Profit to Capital A/C	GL/1	5,000 -					
				12,000 -					12,000 -

CAPITAL, A. BELL (Personal)									A/C ref: GL/1
1970 Dec	31	Balance c/d	c/d	24,000 -	1970 Jan	1	CASH	CB/1	19,000 -
					Dec	31	Net profit from Profit & Loss A/C	GL/9	5,000 -
				24,000 -					24,000 -
					1971 Jan	1	Balance	b/d	24,000 -

It can be seen that the balances in all the nominal accounts are eliminated by the entries made in transferring them to the revenue accounts, leaving the nominal accounts cleared to take new entries during the next trading period. It can also be seen that the balances in the remaining real and personal accounts are either debit balances representing assets, including monies owned, or credit balances representing the liabilities of the business to its proprietor and its creditors. These final balances are listed below.

	£	DEBITS £	CREDITS £
Motor Delivery Vans	2,000 +	2,000	
Warehouse Fixtures	1,700 +	1,700	
Plant and Machinery	4,000 +	4,000	
Premises	15,000 +	15,000	
S. Milkin Ltd.	500 +	500	
C. Elling Ltd.	500 +	500	
J. Baking & Company	1,000 +	1,000	
H. Greenacre Ltd.	5,000 +	5,000	
C. Mending & Co. Ltd.	12,000 -		12,000
G. Greening Ltd.	6,000 -		6,000
Cash at bank	990 +	990	
Cash in hand	10 +	10	
Office Furniture & Fittings	300 +	300	
Capital, A. Bell	24,000 -		24,000
Stock at 31st December 1970	11,000 +	11,000	
	NIL	42,000	42,000

The liability of the business to the proprietor in respect of his original investment plus the net profit made, must be equal to the net value of the possessions of the business (net assets or net worth of the business). If the *credit* balance of £24,000 in A. Bell's capital account is separated from the remainder of the final balances, the difference between the remaining debit balances and credit balances is a *debit* of £24,000.

In order to present this state of affairs in the Balance Sheet the final balances are divided into groups, each group having a particular significance of its own.

i)	CAPITAL ACCOUNT, A. Bell			£24,000 -
ii)	FIXED ASSET ACCOUNTS:-			
	Premises		£15,000 +	
	Warehouse Fixtures		1,700 +	
	Plant & Machinery		4,000 +	
	Office Furniture & Fittings		300 +	
	Motor Delivery Vans		2,000 +	£23,000 +
iii)	CURRENT ASSET ACCOUNTS:-			
	Stock		£11,000 +	
	Sundry Debtors' Accounts:-			
	S. Milkin Ltd.	£ 500		
	C. Elling Ltd.	500		
	J. Baking & Company	1,000		
	H. Greenacre Ltd.	5,000	7,000 +	
	Cash at bank	990		
	Cash in hand	10	1,000 +	£19,000 +
iv)	CURRENT LIABILITY ACCOUNTS:-			
	Sundry Creditors' Accounts:-			
	C. Mending & Co.Ltd.	£12,000		
	G. Greening Ltd.	6,000		£18,000 -
				NIL

From these groupings the final balances were listed in the Balance Sheet as follows:

A. BELL

BALANCE SHEET AS AT 31st DECEMBER 1970

	£	£	£
CURRENT ASSETS			
Stock		11,000	
Sundry Debtors		7,000	
Cash at bank	900		
Cash in hand	10	1,000	19,000
CURRENT LIABILITIES			
Sundry Creditors			18,000
NET CURRENT ASSETS			1,000
FIXED ASSETS			
Premises		15,000	
Warehouse Fixtures		1,700	
Office Furniture & Fittings		300	
Plant & Machinery		4,000	
Motor Delivery Vans		2,000	23,000
TOTAL NET ASSETS (NET WORTH)			24,000
Represented by:-			
CAPITAL, A.BELL			24,000

This Balance Sheet showed that the total capital invested in Mr Bell's business by Mr Bell at the end of the first year of trading was £24,000, and that of this amount, £23,000 was tied up in fixed assets and £1,000 was available to work with. The amount by which the monies flowing inwards from the current assets, exceeds in total the total of monies flowing outwards in meeting the current liabilities, (the net current assets) is known as the *working capital.*

The figures used in the construction of the accounts and Balance Sheet for Mr Bell's business for 1970 have been condensed into the basic framework of accounts illustrated in Chapter 2. They should be studied in relation to that framework and to the mathematical formula depicted in Chapter 1 and the Introduction which precedes Chapter 1.

As a result of keeping the principles and practice illustrated for the first year of trading as brief and uncomplicated as practicable, the example used is open to criticism as not being fully realistic on three main grounds:

(i) It is unlikely that a business could operate without using electricity but no expense for heat and light has been shown.
(ii) A business possessing a motor van would incur expenses in running it. These have not been included.
(iii) Some charge must be made in the revenue accounts of all businesses to take into account losses incurred as a result of the ageing and/or wear of fixed assets, and the fixed assets must be reduced in value accordingly. This has not been done.

In the example used for the second year of trading, the costs of heat and light and of running the motor vans are included, and adjustments are made for depreciation in the value of fixed assets.

The detailed entries in respect of the individual transactions which took place are not examined or illustrated. They followed the same principles and practice as have been fully explained and illustrated for the first year of trading. Instead, the Trial Balance which was compiled from the accounts after all transactions has been entered and before the revenue accounts were made up is shown, and only the work required to complete the final accounts and construct the Balance Sheet, including the adjustments for depreciation, is illustrated and commented upon.

This Trial Balance is illustrated in both the traditional form and the vertical form in which it would appear on a machine or computer listing. It is important for the student to learn to identify each balance as a debit or as a credit when no indication other than its title is given, and to understand exactly what it represents. There are, however, a few balances which cannot be identified as debits or credits by their titles alone. An example is the balance in the Profit and Loss Account before such balance has been transferred to the Capital Account of the proprietor. If this balance represents a profit it must be described as 'Profit and Loss Account-credit balance', whereas if it represented a loss it must be described as 'Profit and Loss Account-debit balance'.

The entries in the revenue accounts are illustrated, but with the exception of the Stock Account and the accounts in which the provisions for depreciation are recorded, the corresponding opposite entries in the nominal accounts are not illustrated. The student should train himself to imagine these when preparing revenue accounts from trial balance.

A. Bell
TRIAL BALANCE
as at 31st December, 1971

	£	p		DEBITS £	p	CREDITS £	p
Premises	15,000	-	+	15,000	-		
Warehouse Fixtures	1,700	-	+	1,700	-		
Office Fixtures and Fittings	300	-	+	300	-		
Plant and Machinery	4,000	-	+	4,000	-		
Motor Delivery Vans	2,000	-	+	2,000	-		
Purchases	80,000	-	+	80,000	-		
Stock at 31st December 1970	11,000	-	+	11,000	-		
Sales	101,485	-	-			101,485	-
Motor Van Running Expenses	750	-	+	750	-		
Publicity	268	-	+	268	-		
Salaries	11,015	-	+	11,015	-		
Rates	200	-	+	200	-		
Heat and Light	300	-	+	300	-		
Telephones	272	-	+	272	-		
Stationery	75	-	+	75	-		
Postage	56	-	+	56	-		
Sundry Expenses	44	-	+	44	-		
Bank Charges	5	-	+	5	-		
Sundry debtors	16,000	-	+	16,000	-		
Sundry credtors	20,000	-	-			20,000	-
Cash at bank	2,486	-	+	2,486	-		
Cash in hand	14	-	+	14	-		
Capital, A. Bell	24,000	-	-			24,000	-
	NIL			145,485	-	145,485	-

The stock of goods on hand at 31st December 1971, was valued at £19,515.

It was decided that the premises were more likely to increase (appreciate) in value than to decrease (depreciate) in value in the foreseeable future and that, consequently, no adjustment to the value of this asset would be made in the accounts. As each of the remaining fixed assets would have a limited life, varying in length according to its nature, it would be necessary, each year of its life, to account for the loss incurred as a result of its drop in value, so that, by the end of its life, the whole of its cost would be taken into account in calculating profits in the revenue accounts, and its value in the accounts reduced to nil. It was decided that an equal proportion of the cost of each asset would be taken into account each year of its life, and to this end the life of each asset was estimated. The result was as follows:

	COST £	LIFE YEARS from 1.1.71	ANNUAL DEPRECIATION £	Percentage of cost
Warehouse Fixtures	1,700	10	170	10%
Office Furniture and Fittings	300	20	15	5%
Plant and Machinery	4,000	8	500	12½%
Motor Delivery Vans	2,000	4	500	25%

From the Trial Balance and the above information the final accounts for Mr Bell's second year of trading were made up and the Balance Sheet listed. These are also illustrated in both traditional and vertical forms.

TRADING AND PROFIT & LOSS ACCOUNT FOR THE YEAR ENDED 31st DECEMBER 1971, A/C ref: GL/8 &

		£				£
Stock at 1st Jan 1971	GL/7	11,000	-	Sales	NL/6	101,485
Purchases	NL/5	80,000	-	Stock at 31st Dec 1971	GL/7	19,515
Gross Profit	c/d	30,000	-			
		121,000	-			121,000
Salaries	NL/7	11,015	-	Gross profit	b/d	30,000
Rates	NL/10	200	-			
Telephones	NL/8	272	-			
Heat & Light	NL/11	300	-			
Stationery	NL/2	75	-			
Postage	NL/3	56	-			
Sundry Expenses	NL/4	44	-			
Bank Charges	NL/9	5	-			
Motor Van Expenses	NL/12	750	-			
Publicity	NL/13	268	-			
Depreciation:-						
Warehouse Fixtures	GL/10	170	-			
Office Fixtures and Fittings	GL/11	15	-			
Plant & Machinery	GL/12	500	-			
Motor Vans	GL/13	500	-			
Net Profit to Capital Account	GL/1	15,830	-			
		30,000	-			30,000

It should be noted that when final accounts are presented, the information which they contain should be shown in such a way as to avoid the need for further calculations to disclose the maximum amount of information, and to avoid, so far as is possible, figures which have no significance. In the account form illustrated above, the totals of £121,000 on the trading section have no meaning other than as a balancing factor to equalise the two sides of the account. Furthermore, an additional calculation is required to find the cost of the goods which have actually been sold. The recommended method when the account form is used for the trading section is as follows:

TRADING ACCOUNT FOR THE YEAR ENDED 31ST DECEMBER 1971

	£			£
Stock 1st January 1971	11,000	Sales		101,485
Purchases	80,000			
	91,000			
Stock 31st December 1971	19,515			
Cost of goods sold	71,485			
Gross Profit c/d	30,000			
	101,485			101,485
	=======			=======
		Gross Profit	b/d	30,000

A credit (−) deducted instead of added in the debit side produces the same net result as is obtained by adding it in the credit (−) side. Likewise, a debit (+) deducted instead of added in the credit side produces the same net result as is obtained by adding it in the debit side.

The same principle applies to the presentation of the liabilities and assets in the Balance Sheet where, for instance, the current liabilities are best listed next to the current assets in the calculation and disclosure of the Net Current Assets or Working Capital, as shown in the vertical form illustrated on page 57.

TRADING AND PROFIT AND LOSS ACCOUNT FOR THE YEAR ENDED
31st DECEMBER 1971
(A/C ref: GL/8 & 9)

		£		£	
Sales	NL/6			101,485	-
Stock at 1st Jan 1971	GL/7	11,000	-		
Purchases	NL/5	80,000	-		
		91,000	-		
Stock at 31st Dec 1971	GL/7	19,515	-		
Cost of goods sold				71,485	-
Gross profit				30,000	-
Salaries	NL/7	11,015	-		
Rates	NL/10	200	-		
Telephones	NL/8	272	-		
Heat & Light	NL/11	300	-		
Stationery	NL/2	75	-		
Postage	NL/3	56	-		
Sundry Expenses	NL/4	44	-		
Bank Charges	NL/9	5	-		
Motor Van Expenses	NL/12	750	-		
Publicity	NL/13	268	-		
Depreciation:-					
Warehouse Fixtures	GL/10	170	-		
Office Fixtures & Fittings	GL/11	15	-		
Plant & Machinery	GL/12	500	-		
Motor Vans	GL/13	500	-	14,170	-
Net profit to Capital A/c	GL/1			15,830	-

The balances in the nominal accounts at 31st December 1971, resulting from transactions which took place during 1971, were eliminated when they were transferred to the revenue accounts. The closing entries in the nominal accounts are not illustrated.

The balance of £11,000 in the Stock Account, brought forward from 31st December *1970* and representing the value of the goods possessed at that date, was eliminated when it was transferred to the Trading Account for the year ended 31st December *1971* as the stock at the *start* of that year's trading. A new debit entry of £19,515 was made on the Stock Account and credited to the Trading Account to complete, in conjunction with the stock at the start and the purchases, the calculation of the cost of the goods sold during 1971. The entries in the Stock Account are illustrated.

No new fixed assets were acquired during 1971. Consequently, the balances in these real accounts remained the same at 31st December 1971 as they were at 31st December 1970, and are not re-illustrated. To record the reductions in their values, as described on page 59, and to charge these reductions in the revenue accounts, a new account for each asset was opened in the General Ledger and credited with the amount of depreciation debited to the Profit and Loss Account. The effect of these double entries was to reduce both the net profit and the value of the fixed assets in the accounts by the same amount. These new accounts are illustrated.

The accounts in which depreciations are credited are entitled 'Provision for Depreciation of ....'. The reduced value of a fixed asset is arrived at by deducting from its original cost, as recorded in its real account, the total to date of the depreciation, as recorded in its provision for depreciation account. Each year, its cost remains unchanged in its asset account, but the credit balance in its provision for depreciation account is increased by the additional annual depreciation charged in the revenue accounts.

The Capital Account is also illustrated, to show the transfer of the net profit made during 1971 from the credit of the Profit and Loss Account to the credit of Mr A. Bell.

STOCK (real)									A/C ref: GL/7		
1970						1971					
DEC	31	TRADING A/C	GL/8	11,000	-	Dec	31	Trading A/C	GL/8	11,000	-
1971											
Dec	31	Trading A/C	GL/8	19,515	-						

PROVISION FOR DEPRECIATION OF WAREHOUSE FIXTURES									A/C ref: GL/10		
						1971					
						Dec	31	Profit & Loss A/C	GL/9	170	-

PROVISION FOR DEPRECIATION OF OFFICE FIXTURES & FITTINGS									A/C ref: GL/11		
						1971					
						Dec	31	Profit & Loss A/C	GL/9	15	-

PROVISION FOR DEPRECIATION OF PLANT AND MACHINERY									A/C ref: GL/12		
						1971					
						Dec	31	Profit & Loss A/C	GL/9	500	-

PROVISION FOR DEPRECIATION OF MOTOR DELIVERY VANS									A/C ref: GL/13		
						1971					
						Dec	31	Profit & Loss A/C	GL/9	500	-

CAPITAL, A. BELL (Personal)									A/C ref: GL/1		
1970						1970					
DEC	31	BALANCE	c/d	24,000	-	JAN	1	CASH	CB/1	19,000	-
						DEC	31	NET PROFIT FOR YEAR	GL/9	5,000	-
				24,000	-					24,000	-
1971						1971					
Dec	31	Balance	c/d	39,830	-	Jan	1	BALANCE	b/d	24,000	-
						Dec	31	Net profit for year	GL/9	15,830	-
				39,830	-					39,830	-
						1972					
						Jan	1	Balance	b/d	39,830	-

The final balances outstanding in the accounts of Mr Bell's business *after* the revenue accounts had been completed and all the relevant entries in the accounts had been made, are listed below in both vertical and traditional forms:

	£	p		DEBITS £	p	CREDITS £	p
Premises	15,000	-	+	15,000	-		
Warehouse Fixtures	1,700	-	+	1,700	-		
Office Fixtures and Fittings	300	-	+	300	-		
Plant and Machinery	4,000	-	+	4,000	-		
Motor Delivery Vans	2,000	-	+	2,000	-		
Sundry Debtors	16,000	-	+	16,000	-		
Sundry Creditors	20,000	-	-			20,000	-
Cash at Bank	2,486	-	+	2,486	-		
Cash in hand	14	-	+	14	-		
Provision for Depreciation:-							
Warehouse Fixtures	170	-	-			170	-
Office Fixtures and Fittings	15	-	-			15	-
Plant and Machinery	500	-	-			500	-
Motor Delivery Vans	500	-	-			500	-
Stock at 31st December 1971	19,515	-	+	19,515	-		
Capital, A. Bell	39,830	-	-			38,830	-
	NIL			61,015	-	61,015	-

These balances were listed in the Balance Sheet as follows:

A. BELL

BALANCE SHEET AS AT 31ST DECEMBER 1971

	£	£	£
CURRENT ASSETS			
Stock		19,515	
Sundry Debtors		16,000	
Cash at Bank	2,486		
Cash in hand	14	2,500	38,015
CURRENT LIABILITIES			
Sundry Creditors			20,000
NET CURRENT ASSETS (Working Capital)			18,015
FIXED ASSETS			
Premises at cost		15,000	
Warehouse Fixtures at cost	1,700		
Less depreciation to date	170	1,530	
Ofice Furniture and Fixtures at cost	300		
Less depreciation to date	15	285	
Plant and Machinery at cost	4,000		
Less depreciation to date	500	3,500	
Motor Delivery Vans at cost	2,000		
Less depreciation to date	500	1,500	21,815
TOTAL NET ASSETS (Net worth)			39,830
Represented by:-			
CAPITAL, A. BELL			39,830

This Balance Sheet showed that during 1971, as a result of the profits made and left in the business, the amount invested in the business by Mr Bell had increased to £39,830. Of this amount, £21,815 was tied up in fixed assets (reduced in value by depreciation), and the working capital had been increased to £18,015. It should be noted that the amount invested in stocks was greater than the working capital and consequently the working capital could not be considered more than sufficient for the prompt payment of the creditors.

If Mr Bell had withdrawn money from the business during the year the working capital would have been reduced. The cash at bank would have been reduced, thereby reducing the current assets, the net current assets, the total net assets and the capital invested, equally.

In traditional form the Balance Sheet would have been laid out as follows:

BALANCE SHEET AS AT 31st DECEMBER, 1971

	£		£	£	£
CAPITAL	39,830	FIXED ASSETS			
		Premises at cost			15,000
CURRENT LIABILITIES		Warehouses Fixtures at cost		1,700	
Sundry Creditors	20,000	Less Depreciation to date		170	1,530
		Office Furniture and Fixtures at cost		300	
		Less Depreciation to date		15	285
		Plant & Machinery at cost		4,000	
		Less Depreciation to date		500	3,500
		Motor Delivery Vans at cost		2,000	
		Less Depreciation to date		500	1,500
					21,815
		CURRENT ASSETS			
		Stock		19,515	
		Sundry Debtors		16,000	
		Cash at Bank	2,486		
		Cash in Hand	14	2,500	38,015
	59,830				59,830

EXERCISES

1. From the following trial balance of J. Fireman, prepare the Trading and Profit and Loss Account and compile the Balance Sheet.

TRIAL BALANCE 31 DECEMBER 19..

	£	£
Cash at bank	1,290	
Capital, J. Fireman 1 January 19.. ...		9,500
Office furniture	1,000	
Sales		16,240
Motor Van	500	
Rent	750	
Purchases	15,040	
Light and Heat	262	
Sundry debtors and creditors	6,750	926
General expenses	1,074	
	26,666	26,666

The stock on hand at 31 December 19. . was valued at £1,510. No adjustments are required for depreciation of fixed assets.

2. At the close of the second year of trading, J. Fireman's accounts contained the following balances:

TRIAL BALANCE 31 DECEMBER 19.1

	£	£
Stock, 31 December 19..	1,510	
Capital		10,124
Purchases	13,450	
Rent	750	
Light and Heat	295	
General expenses	1,081	
Sales		15,407
Office furniture	1,000	
Motor Van	500	
Sundry debtors	8,326	
Sundry creditors		1,733
Office salaries	1,200	
Bank overdraft		848
	28,112	28,112

Prepare the Trading and Profit and Loss Account for the year ended 31 December 19.1 and compile the Balance Sheet as at 31 December 19.1. The stock on hand at 31 December 19.1 was valued at £1,953. Ignore depreciation of fixed assets.

3. The following balances were extracted from the accounts of G. Meadows preparatory to making up the final accounts for the year ended 30 June 19.1.

	£
Capital	18,550
Freehold premises	10,000
Stock 1 July 19..	7,232
Motor Van Expenses	487
Office fixtures and fittings	1,400
Motor Vans	1,500
Rates	164
Sundry debtors	11,216
Sales	67,311
Postage and Stationery	105
Light and Heat	233
Salaries	8,009
Sundry creditors	13,405
Telephone expenses	182
Purchases	56,900
Cash at Bank	1,609
Cash in Hand	32
Sundry expenses	53
Publicity	144

Stock at 30 June 19.1 was valued at £12,277.

You are required to draw up the Trading and Profit and Loss Account for the year ended 30 June 19.1 and the Balance Sheet as at that date. Ignore depreciation of fixed assets.

4. The following balances appeared in the Trial Balance of a sole trader as at 31 December 19. ., the closing date of the first year of trading.

TRIAL BALANCE 31 DECEMBER 19.. (EXTRACT)

	£
Plant and machinery	6,000
Warehouse Fixtures	2,000
Motor Van	600

It was decided that the fixed assets, all of which were bought ex bank 1 January 19. ., were to be reduced in value by an equal amount annually and that the rates of depreciation to be used for this purpose were to be: Plant and Machinery 10% per annum, Office Fixtures 5% per annum and Motor Van 25% per annum.

(*a*) Show the entries in the fixed asset accounts and the accounts for the provisions for depreciation, as they would have appeared therein after the Profit and Loss Account had been compiled.

(*b*) Compile an extract showing how the relevant items would have been listed in the Balance Sheet as at 31 December 19. .

5. The final balances outstanding in the accounts of the business of B. R. Blackson, after the revenue accounts had been completed for the year ended 30 September 19.1, were as follows:

	£
Premises	30,000
Fixtures and fittings	4,000
Plant	8,000
Motor Vans	4,000
Sundry debtors	32,000
Sundry creditors	50,000
Bank overdraft	5,028
Cash in hand	28
Provisions for depreciation:	
Fixtures and fittings	400
Plant	1,000
Motor Vans	1,000
Stock 30 September 19.1	29,154
Capital, B.R.Blackson:	
Balance 1 October 19..	43,329
Profit for the year	6,425

You are required to compile the Balance Sheet as at 30 September 19.1 in both traditional and vertical forms.

6. J. S. Littleman commenced business 1 April 19.. and the following Trial Balance was extracted from his business accounts as at 31 March 19.1.

TRIAL BALANCE 31 MARCH 19.1.	£	£
Bank overdraft		7,000
Cash in hand	158	
Purchases	24,294	
Sales		29,316
Sundry debtors and creditors	4,920	3,793
Plant and machinery	1,600	
Fixtures and fittings	1,500	
Motor vehicles	1,000	
Rent and rates	992	
Postage and stationery	104	
Salaries	5,381	
Telephone expenses	92	
General expenses	77	
Vehicle running expenses	991	
Capital, J.S.Littleman		1,000
	41,109	41,109

The fixed assets were acquired 1 April 19.. The stock at 31 March 19.1 was valued at £4,522.

You are required to make up the Trading and Profit and Loss Account for the year ended 31 March 19.1, including charges for depreciation at the rates of $12\frac{1}{2}$% for Plant and Machinery, 10% for Fixtures and Fittings and 20% for Motor Vehicles. You are also required to compile the Balance Sheet as at 31 March 19.1.

CHAPTER 7

Drawings

Some sole traders and partners fail because they do not fully understand the effects on their finances and profits of withdrawing money and value in other forms from the business. Often, a fixed amount is withdrawn weekly or monthly without consideration of how much profit has to be, or can be, made to cover it, as though they are employees receiving wages or salaries.

A *sole trader* is a person who is running a business as its owner and is personally liable for all its liabilities. A *partnership* is owned by two or more persons each of whom is individually and together with the other partner or partners liable for all liabilities incurred by the business. In both cases such persons are not employees earning wages or salaries unless and until such time as the business is turned into a *limited company*.

Value may be withdrawn from a business into private ownership and for private use, by its proprietor, in different forms. Such withdrawals, in accounting, are known as DRAWINGS. The following points should be understood:

(*a*) Drawings are PERSONAL. They reduce the debt owing by a business to its proprietor.
(*b*) Drawings are not expenses or losses, even though they reduce both total net assets and capital liability. They are withdrawals OF profit or, if insufficient profit is made to cover them, withdrawals of capital invested.
(*c*) The value withdrawn is no longer in the business for its own use or for resale; it has passed outside the business even though it has passed to the owner of the business.
(*d*) The reduction in the value held by the business must be recorded in the account for the particular kind of value withdrawn.
(*e*) Whatever kind of value possessed by the business may be reduced or eliminated by drawings, the drawings will always also equally reduce capital liability.

The most common form of drawings is money, but value other than money may be withdrawn. If money is withdrawn from the bank of the business by its proprietor, the Cash Book is credited to record the reduction in the asset of cash at bank, and the Capital Account is debited to record the reduction in the capital liability. If money is withdrawn from cash in hand, the Petty Cash Book is credited and the Capital Account is debited. If the value of the space occupied by the business is reduced by private occupation of a part thereof, by its proprietor, the value of that part is credited to the Rent Payable Account and debited to the Capital Account. Should the proprietor take a motor car out of the business into private ownership, the Motor Cars Account would be credited, and the Capital Account would be debited. If goods held for resale are withdrawn, the Purchases Account is credited and the Capital Account is debited.

Some additional treatment is required in the accounts when a fixed asset which has had depreciation charged against it, such as a motor car, is withdrawn into private ownership by the proprietor of a business. This, however, will be understood when a further study of depreciation and the disposal of fixed assets is undertaken.

When dealing with drawings, the student must be careful to avoid possible confusion in connection with purchases, stocks and sales. He should, at this stage, revise his study of Chapter 5, which deals with goods traded, stock and gross profit.

The Purchases Account accumulates the total cost of ALL goods taken into a business and either sold to clients for a profit, or kept available for sale to clients, during the WHOLE of a trading period. If any such goods are removed from availability for sale to clients, either by return to their supplier, by being taken out from the business by its proprietor, or as a result of internal use or consumption within the business itself, the COST thereof must be deducted from the total PURCHASES. Drawings of goods which were previously intended for sale must, therefore, be recorded as a credit (−) entry in the Purchases Account. The corresponding debit (+) entry will, as previously explained, be made in the Capital Account.

The Stock Account records the cost, or market value, of the goods REMAINING IN a business on the last day ONLY of a trading period, at which time all deliveries of goods to clients as a result of sales, all returns of goods to their suppliers, all withdrawals of goods by the proprietor, and all transfers of goods from stock for internal use or consumption, have already taken place. The cost of such withdrawals of goods from availability for sale is automatically excluded from the figure for stock at close. The stock at the start of a trading period is exactly the same stock as the stock at the close of the previous trading period. Once its value has been correctly established as shown in the accounts at the close of one trading period, it cannot change for that date, and must be used without alteration as the stock at the start of the following trading period. Drawings of goods must NOT, therefore, be deducted from stocks.

The Sales Account accumulates the total SELLING VALUE of all goods which pass out from a business as a result of sales to clients, for a profit, during the whole of a trading period. The selling value not only includes the cost value of the goods parted with, but also includes the value of all other expenses which is recovered from the clients in the selling value, plus a profit or less a loss as the case may be. Value withdrawn from availability FOR sales cannot increase sales. Drawings of goods must NOT, therefore, be added to sales. The only circumstances which could provide an exception to this rule would be such as required the proprietor to account for goods withdrawn at a higher value than cost, in which case some value in addition to the cost of the goods would pass out from the business with the goods, bringing an element of profit into the transaction. In the unlikely event of such an exceptional case, the transaction would then be treated as a sale; a credit (−) entry would be made in the Sales Account and a debit (+) entry in the Capital Account.

When there are a number of transactions of the same kind to be debited or credited to a main account during the course of a trading period, it is an advantage to accumulate them in a subsidiary or 'transit' account so that their total at the close of trading period may be transferred to the main account in one amount.

This treatment makes the total of such transactions readily available at any time. The ascertainment of such a total would otherwise require an analysis of the entries in the main account.

To achieve this result in respect of drawings, a personal account with the proprietor, which is subsidiary to the Capital Account, is used. This is called the DRAWINGS ACCOUNT.

The debit (+) entries required for all withdrawals of value from the business by its proprietor are entered in this account under the dates on which they occur during the trading period. At the close of the trading period, when the final accounts are made up, the total of the entries for the period is transferred from the debit of the Drawings Account to the debit of the Capital Account with one double entry. The Drawings Account is thus cleared to take new entries during the following trading period.

The credit (−) entries in respect of drawings are not affected by the special treatment of the debit (+) entries. The credit (−) entries are dealt with in the manner already described.

After the final accounts of Mr Bell's business had been made up for the year ended 31 December 1971, as previously illustrated, the following matters were brought to light.

The banks supply to their clients, at regular intervals, statements showing all the amounts of money paid into and withdrawn from their bank accounts. These statements are used by those who have bank accounts to check that their own records of bank transactions agree with the records of their bankers.

When the entries in the Cash Book for Mr Bell's business were checked with those appearing on the bank's statement, it was found that on the last day of each month during the year Mr Bell had transferred £100 from the bank account of the business to his private bank account. No entries had been made to record these transactions in the accounts of the business.

Also, on 15 June 1971, Mr Bell had taken out from the business for private use, goods which the business had purchased at a cost of £115 for sale to clients.

These errors had to be corrected in the accounts, and revised final accounts produced. Also a corrected balance sheet had to be listed.

The Cash Book was corrected was follows:

CASH BOOK (Real)												A/C ref: CB/1	
1972 JAN	1	BALANCE	B/d	2,486	-	1971 Dec	31	Drawings for year	GL/14	1,200	-		
						"	"	Balance	C/d	1,286	-		
				2,486	-					2,486	-		
1972 Jan	1	Balance	B/d	1,286	-								

If each individual transfer of cash had originally been recorded on the date on which it occurred, the Cash Book would have contained twelve additional credit (−) entries during the trading period, and the final balance on this account at the end of the year would have been the correct figure of £1,286.

A Drawings Account was opened, debit (+) entries made therein for 1971, and closed with a transfer of the total drawings to the Capital Account, as follows:

DRAWINGS, A. BELL (Personal)								A/C ref: GL/14	
1971					1971				
June	15	Purchases	NL/5	115 -	Dec	31	Capital	GL/1	1,315 -
Dec	31	Cash	CB/1	1,200 -					
				1,315 -					1,315 -

If the individual drawings had been correctly recorded on their appropriate dates, the Drawings Account would have appeared as follows:

DRAWINGS, A.BELL (Personal)								A/c ref: GL/14	
1971					1971				
Jan	31	Cash	CB/1	100 -	Dec	31	CAPITAL	GL/1	1,315 -
Feb	28	"	CB/1	100 -					
Mch	31	"	CB/1	100 -					
Apr	30	"	CB/1	100 -					
May	31	"	CB/1	100 -					
Jun	15	Purchases	NL/5	115 -					
"	30	Cash	CB/1	100 -					
Jul	31	"	CB/1	100 -					
Aug	31	"	CB/1	100 -					
Sep	30	"	CB/1	100 -					
Oct	31	"	CB/1	100 -					
Nov	30	"	CB/1	100 -					
Dec	31	"	CB/1	100 -					
				1,315 -					1,315 -

The corrections to the Capital Account are illustrated after the corrections to the Purchases Account and the Trading and Profit and Loss Account. The Purchases Account for 1971 was corrected as follows:-

PURCHASES (Nominal)								A/C ref: NL/5	
1971					1971				
JAN to DEC	1 31	ENTRIES MADE DURING 1971		VARIOUS AMOUNTS	DEC	31	TRADING ACCOUNT	GL/8	80,000 -
				80,000 -					80,000 -
Dec	31	Trading Account	GL/8	115 -	Dec	31	Drawings	GL/14	115 -

It will be realised that the total of £80,000 in the debit (+) side of the Purchases Account would have been made up by a number of separate debit (+) entries in respect of various transactions which took place during 1971, and which were not detailed in the original example. It must also be realised that if the drawings in goods had been credited to the Purchases Account at the proper time, the balance which was transferred to the Trading Account, in the first place, would have been £79,885 instead of £80,000.

As the stock figure at 31 December 1971 was the value of only those goods which were in possession of the business at that date, and the drawings in goods had already been taken out when the stock was counted, the subsequent discovery of the drawings had no effect on the stock figure. The cost of the goods withdrawn had inadvertently been included in the purchases total as part of the cost of the goods sold, as a result of which both the gross and net profits were understated.

A corrected Trading and Profit and Loss Account was made up as follows:

TRADING AND PROFIT AND LOSS ACCOUNT
FOR THE YEAR ENDED 31 DECEMBER 1971
(A/C ref: GL/8 & 9)

		£	p	£	p
SALES	NL/6			101,485	-
STOCK AT 1 JANUARY 1971	GL/7	11,000	-		
Purchases	NL/5	79,885	-		
		90,885	-		
STOCK AT 31 DECEMBER 1971	GL/7	19,515	-		
Cost of goods sold				71,370	-
Gross profit				30,115	-
SALARIES	NL/7	11,015	-		
RATES	NL/10	200	-		
TELEPHONES	NL/8	272	-		
HEAT AND LIGHT	NL/11	300	-		
STATIONERY	NL/2	75	-		
POSTAGE	NL/3	56	-		
SUNDRY EXPENSES	NL/4	44	-		
BANK CHARGES	NL/9	5	-		
MOTOR VAN EXPENSES	NL/12	750	-		
PUBLICITY	NL/13	268	-		
DEPRECIATION:-					
WAREHOUSE FIXTURES	GL/10	170	-		
OFFICE FIXTURES AND FITTINGS	GL/11	15	-		
PLANT AND MACHINERY	GL/12	500	-		
MOTOR VANS	GL/13	500	-	14,170	-
Net profit to Capital Account	GL/1			15,945	-

The Capital Account was corrected as follows:

CAPITAL, A. BELL (Personal) A/C ref: GL/1

1971						1972					
Dec	31	Drawings	GL/14	1,315	-	JAN	1	BALANCE	B/D	39,830	-
"	"	Balance	c/d	38,630	-	1971 Dec	31	Additional profit 1971	GL/9	115	-
				39,945	-					39,945	-
						1972					
						Jan	1	Balance	b/d	38,630	-

If the drawings had not been omitted from the accounts when they were originally compiled, the Capital Account would have appeared as follows:-

CAPITAL, A. BELL (Personal) A/C ref: GL/1

1971						1971					
DEC	31	DRAWINGS	GL/14	1,315	-	JAN	1	BALANCE	B/D	24,000	-
"	"	BALANCE	c/c	38,630	-	Dec	31	Net profit for year	GL/9	15,945	-
				39,945	-					39,945	-
						1972					
						Jan	1	BALANCE	b/d	38,630	-

The corrected balance sheet appeared as follows:

BALANCE SHEET AS AT 31 DECEMBER 1971

	£	£	£
CURRENT ASSETS			
STOCK		19,515	
SUNDRY DEBTORS		16,000	
Cash at Bank	1,286		
CASH IN HAND	14	1,300	36,815
CURRENT LIABILITIES			
SUNDRY CREDITORS			20,000
Net Current Assets (Working Capital)			16,815
FIXED ASSETS			
PREMISES AT COST		15,000	
WAREHOUSE FIXTURES AT COST	1,700		
LESS DEPRECIATION TO DATE	170	1,530	
OFFICE FURNITURE AND FIXTURES AT COST	300		
LESS DEPRECIATION TO DATE	15	285	
PLANT AND MACHINERY AT COST	4,000		
LESS DEPRECIATION TO DATE	500	3,500	
MOTOR DELIVERY VANS AT COST	2,000		
LESS DEPRECIATION TO DATE	500	1,500	21,815
Total Net Assets (Net worth)			38,630
Financed by:-			
Capital, A. Bell			38,630

The difference between the profit shown in the first Trading and Profit and Loss Account produced for Mr Bell's business for 1971, and the profit shown in the corrected amount, is the result of the error which was made by the inclusion in the cost of the goods sold, of goods which, in fact, were not part of the sales.

It is important that the student should realise, from the example and explanations given, that drawings in CASH do not affect the calculations of profit or loss, whereas drawings in GOODS originally intended for resale DO affect such calculations. Drawings of any kind are not costs or expenses and cannot be charged against sales in the revenue accounts. It is because the figure used in the Trading Account, for purchases, in the calculation of profit, is the total of all goods received for resale, that the profit will be UNDER-stated if the cost of goods withdrawn is not deducted therefrom. All costs and expenses must be reduced by any withdrawals therefrom before they are debited to the revenue accounts. To put it another way, costs and expenses will be OVER-charged in the revenue accounts if they are not reduced by the cost of any withdrawals therefrom.

Also, in addition to understanding how drawings are dealt with in the accounts, the student should note how drawings equally reduce the current assets, the working capital, the total net assets, and the capital liability.

The student should also satisfy himself as to the reason why, in comparing the corrected balance sheet, as illustrated on page 72 (this page) with the original balance sheet shown on page 63 of Chapter 6, he sees that the corrections made by bringing into account drawings totalling £1,315 have resulted in an overall reduction, in both capital liability and total net assets, of only £1,200.

The overstatement of the capital liability, caused by not deducting therefrom the drawings of £115 in goods, was counterbalanced by the understatement of the profit added thereto, caused by not deducting the drawings of £115 in goods from the purchases. Consequently, the final balance to the credit of the Capital Account was not erroneously stated as a result of the omission of the drawings in goods, despite their absence from the Drawings Account and the mis-statement of the net profit. On the other side of the accounting equation, the total of net assets was not erroneously stated as a result of the omission of the drawings in goods because the goods withdrawn were automatically excluded from the stock at close, being absent when the stock was counted and valued. If this explanation is not clear to the student, further revision of Chapter 5 should be undertaken.

Because drawings in cash do not affect the calculation of profit or loss, their omission from the accounts does result in an overstatement of both the capital liability and the total net assets. The credit balance on the Capital Account is overstated because the absence of the drawings in cash is not counterbalanced by a shortage of an equal amount of profit. The cash at bank is overstated in the total net assets because it relies on the entries in the Cash Book and not on a physical count.

It should be noted that drawings must be taken into account in any calculation of profit or loss which is based solely on an increase or decrease in capital liability. In the example last illustrated, the calculation of net profit from opening and closing capitals for the year ended 31 December 1971 is as follows:

	£
Capital 31 December 1971 (after drawings deducted)	38,630
Drawings added back	1,315
Capital 31 December 1971 (before drawings deducted)	39,945
Capital 1 January 1971	24,000
Net profit for year ended 31 December 1971	15,945

Finally, the student must realise that all payments made by a business on behalf of its proprietor in settlement of the proprietor's private debts must be charged to the proprietor. Examples of such payments are rent, rates, electricity, gas or private telephone expenses in respect of the proprietor's private residence or affairs, and income tax on the profit made by the business which, in the case of a sole trader or partner, is the private liability of the proprietor.

EXERCISES

1. (*a*) State the equation upon which the mathematical formula for the Double Entry System of Accounting is based.
   (*b*) Show the alternative way in which the Accounting Equation may be stated.

2. Explain the circumstances in which value received remains an asset and the circumstances in which it becomes a cost or expense.

3. Give the reasons why:
   (*a*) gains and profits are credits (−)
   (*b*) costs and expenses are debits (+)
   (*c*) three accounts instead of one only are used for goods traded.

4. Describe the meanings of the following terms and, in each case, state how its value is calculated:
   (*a*) Capital Invested
   (*b*) Total NET Assets
   (*c*) Total Assets
   (*d*) Capital Liability
   (*e*) TOTAL Liabilities.

5. Explain what you understand by Working Capital, how its amount is calculated, why it is important to a business and what is the main danger in a deficiency thereof.

6. Give the two main alternative interpretations of Capital Employed.

7. State the difference between each of the following pairs of items:
   (*a*) Capital Liability and Current liabilities
   (*b*) Fixed Assets and Current Assets
   (*c*) Trial Balance and Balance Sheet
   (*d*) Total Cash possessed and Net Monetary Position
   (*e*) A cash transaction and a credit transaction
   (*f*) Gross profit and net profit.

8. All withdrawals of value from a business by its proprietor must find their way through the Drawings Account to the debit of the Capital Account. State against each of the following withdrawals the account to be credited:
   1. Cash ex bank
   2. Cash ex petty cash
   3. Goods purchased for resale
   4. Private use of motor car which has been included in the motor car running expenses booked by the business.
   5. Private stationery charged in the business accounts.
   6. Private electricity bill, for lighting and heating the proprietor's residence, paid by the business.

9. The balances listed below have been taken from the Trial Balance of a sole trader as at 31 March 19.2.

	£
Capital	2,000
Drawings	960
Sales	30,000
Electricity	170
Purchases	20,000
Stationery	100
Motor Car Expenses	150
Stock	7,000
A. Browney (debtor)	1,000

The following had not been taken into account:

(*a*) Goods purchased for resale costing £15 had been taken by the owner for private use.

(*b*) One third of the motor car expenses was in respect of private use of the car by the owner.

(*c*) Goods returned from client A. Browney for agreed allowances totalling £200 had not been recorded in the relevant nominal account and personal account.

(*d*) The business accounts included payments made by the business on behalf of the owner for:

Personal stationery for private use £4

Electricity consumed at private address £13.

You are required to show the relevant accounts as they appeared after the necessary entries had been made to bring the above matters into account.

10. F. Swimmer was a retailer who purchased his supplies on a cash and carry basis. After all transactions known by his bookkeeper to have taken place during the year ended 31 December 19.3 had been entered in the books, the following balances were extracted:

	£
Capital	9,155
Leasehold premises (premium paid)	5,000
Motor Car	1,800
Stock, 31 December 19.2	2,364
Purchases	20,826
Stationery	32
Cash Sales	25,943
Wages of shop assistants	1,500
Rent	650
Light and Heat	149
Fixtures and fittings	848
Telephone expenses	35
General expenses	62
Motor Car Expenses	177
Cash at Bank	1,655

The following matters had not been taken into account:

Of the motor car expenses charged to the business, £155 had been expended by the owner in private motoring. The owner had withdrawn from the bank account of the business £120 per month throughout the year, and had taken from stock during the year goods costing £71.

You are required to show the balances listed above, as brought down at 31 December 19.3, in the relevant accounts, make the required adjustments and carry down revised balances where necessary therein, take out the Trial Balance, make the final entries to construct the Trading and Profit and Loss Account for the year ended 31 December 19.3 and compile the Balance Sheet as at that date. The stock at 31 December 19.3 was valued at £2,412.
(Ignore depreciation)

ANSWERS TO EXERCISES

CHAPTER 1

1. (*a*) For accounting purposes a business is considered to be an entity which is distinct from its owner, to whom it is accountable. Only that part of the owner's private fortune which is invested in a business is of concern to the business. The amount invested in a business is a private asset of the owner and a liability of the business to its owner. It becomes the capital of the business. Transactions are recorded by a business only in so far as they affect the business and its capital liability to its owner. When an owner takes part in his business, he is acting on behalf of the business and not in his private or personal capacity. His private fortune is only affected in so far as his investment in the business is affected.

(*b*) Every transaction entered into by a business has two aspects. It involves both the parting with value and the receipt of value. The former is treated as credit (−) and the latter as debit (+). In monetary terms, for every transaction, the value parted with is equal to the value received. Both aspects of every transaction are recorded with a double entry consisting of a debit (+) in one account for the value received and a credit (−) in another account for the value parted with. Mathematically, together with the Business Entity Concept, this results in the Accounting Equation, i.e. Total Net Assets − Capital Liability equals NIL.

(*c*) In addition to the ascertainment of profit or loss and the financial state of affairs in accordance with correct accounting principles, the accounts of a business should be designed to provide the maximum possible information relevant to efficient management. It should not dictate management procedure but fulfil management requirements.

2. (a)

A. JAX

CAPITAL — A/C.ref:GL/1

				1970			
				Jan 1	Cash	CB/1	5,000.00

CASH — A/C.ref:CB/1

1970				1970			
Jan 1	Capital	GL/1	5,000.00	Jan 2	Purchases	NL/1	1,000.00
" 4	Sales	NL/2	1,500.00	" 8	Expenses	NL/3	200.00

PURCHASES — A/C.ref:NL/1

1970				1970			
Jan 2	Cash	CB/1	1,000.00				

SALES — A/C.ref:NL/2

				1970			
				Jan 2	Cash	CB/1	1,500.00

EXPENSES — A/C.ref:NL/5

1970							
Jan 8	Cash	CB/1	200.00				

(b) CALCULATION OF PROFIT FOR THE WEEK ENDED 8 JANUARY 1970:

	£	£	
Gains: Sales		1,500	(credit -)
Costs & Expenses:			
Purchases	1,000		(debit +)
Expenses	200	1,200	(debit +)
		300	(credit -)

(c) CALCULATION OF INCREASE IN CAPITAL DURING THE WEEK ENDED 8 JANUARY 1970:-

	£	
Capital introduced 1 January 1970	5,000	(credit -)
Gains	1,500	(credit -)
	6,500	(credit -)
Costs & Expenses	1,200	(debit +)
Capital as at 8 January 1970	5,300	(credit -)
Therefore increase in capital	300	(credit -)

OR, as the net profit has already been calculated:-

	£	
Capital introduced 1 January 1970	5,000	(credit -)
Net profit for the week	300	(credit -)
Capital as at 8 January 1970	5,300	(credit -)
Therefore increase in capital	300	(credit -)

(d) BALANCE SHEET AS AT 8 JANUARY 1970 - A. JAX

CAPITAL	£	CURRENT ASSETS	£
Balance 1 January 1970	5,000.00	Cash	5,300.00
Profit for the week	300.00		
	5,300.00		5,300.00

3. (a) J. BESBY

CAPITAL A/C.ref:GL/1

				1971			
				Mch 1	Cash	CB/1	3,000.00

CASH A/C.ref:CB/1

1971				1971			
Mch 1	Capital	GL/1	3,000.00	Mch 1	Rent	NL/1	20.00
" 4	Sales	NL/3	1,200.00	" 2	Office Fixtures	GL/2	150.00
				" 3	Purchases	NL/2	900.00
				" 5	General Exps	NL/4	50.00

RENT — A/C.ref:NL/1

1971					
Mch 1 Cash	CB/1	20.00			

OFFICE FIXTURES — A/C.ref:GL/2

1971					
Mch 2 Cash	CB/1	150.00			

PURCHASES — A/C.ref:NL/2

1971					
Mch 3 Cash	CB/1	900.00			

SALES — A/C.ref:NL/3

			1971		
			Mch 4 Cash	CB/1	1,200.00

GENERAL EXPENSES — A/C.ref:NL/4

1971					
Mch 5 Cash	CB/1	50.00			

(b) CALCULATION OF TOTAL NET ASSETS AS AT 5 MARCH 1971:-

	£	
Office Fixtures	150	(debit +)
Cash	3,080	(debit +)
Total net assets	3,230	(debit +)

CALCULATION OF CAPITAL LIABILITY AS AT 5 MARCH 1971:-

	£	£	
Capital introduced 1 March 1971		3,000	(credit -)
Gains : Sales		1,200	(credit -)
		4,200	(credit -)
Costs & Expenses			
Purchases	900		
Rent	20		
General Expenses	50	970	(debit +)
Capital 5 March 1971		3,230	(credit -)

OR:-

Capital introduced 1 March 1971		3,000	(credit -)
Gains	1,200		(credit -)
Costs & Expenses	970		(debit +)
Net profit for the week		230	(credit -)
Capital as at 5 March 1971		3,230	(credit -)

4. (a)

A. GLYDER

BALANCE SHEET as at 30 JUNE 1971

	£			£
CAPITAL		FIXED ASSETS		
Balance inc.profit	6,683	Office Fixtures		942
		Machinery		3,261
CURRENT LIABILITIES		Motor Vans		2,500
Creditors	7,432			6,703
		CURRENT ASSETS		
		Stock	1,250	
		Debtors	5,666	
		Cash at Bank	462	
		Cash in Hand	34	7,412
	14,115			14,115

VERTICAL FORM:-

	£	£
CURRENT ASSETS		
Stock		1,250
Debtors		5,666
Cash at Bank	462	
Cash in Hand	34	496
		7,412
CURRENT LIABILITIES		
Creditors		7,432
NET CURRENT LIABILITY (cr -)		20
FIXED ASSETS		
Office Fixtures	942	
Machinery	3,261	
Motor Vans	2,500	6,703
TOTAL NET ASSETS		6,683
Financed by:-		
CAPITAL		
Balance including profit		6,683

(b) **CALCULATION OF PROFIT MADE SINCE ORIGINAL INVESTMENT WAS INTRODUCED:-**

	£
Capital 30 June 1971	6,683
Original Investment	5,000
Net profit	1,683

ANSWERS TO EXERCISES

CHAPTER 2

1. An account which records a physical possession such as cash, stock of unsold goods, or a fixed asset, is judged as being real. An account which records a cost, expense, or gain, is judged as being nominal. An account which records a debt owed by a business or to a business, is judged as being personal. The balances in the real and personal accounts, apart from the personal account of the owner, make up the total net assets or net worth of a business. The balances in the nominal accounts are used to calculate the profit or loss which is added to, or deducted from, the capital liability of a business to its owner.

2. (a) (b) & (c)

NAME OF ACCOUNT	KIND OF ACCOUNT	£ DEBIT (+)	£ CREDIT (-)
Salaries	Nominal	3,129	
Freehold Premises	Real	7,500	
Bank Charges	Nominal	15	
Cash	Real	495	
Purchases of goods	Nominal	24,500	
Postage	Nominal	20	
Petty Cash	Real	5	
Office Fixtures	Real	1,000	
Telephone Expenses	Nominal	61	
Sales of Goods	Nominal		30,000
Rent paid	Nominal	250	
Motor Vans	Real	1,000	
Plant	Real	2,000	
Sundry Debtors	Personal	3,500	
Sundry Creditors	Personal		8,975
Capital	Personal		4,500
		43,475	43,475

ANSWERS TO EXERCISES

CHAPTER 3

1. A.CONY

CAPITAL A/C.ref:GL/1

				19..			
				Jan 1	Cash	CB/1	5,000.00

CASH A/C.ref:CB/1

19..				19..			
Jan 1	Capital	GL/1	5,000.00	Jan 5	Office Furniture	GL/2	250.00
				" 7	R.Supple	PL/1	1,000.00
				" "	Balance	c/d	3,750.00
			5,000.00				5,000.00
Jan 8	Balance	b/d	3,750.00				

PURCHASES A/C.ref:NL/1

19..							
Jan 3	R.Supple	PL/1	2,000.00				

R. SUPPLE A/C.ref:PL/1

19..				19..			
Jan 7	Cash	CB/1	1,000.00	Jan 3	Purchases	NL/1	2,000.00
" "	Balance	c/d	1,000.00				
			2,000.00				2,000.00
				Jan 8	Balance	b/d	1,000.00

OFFICE FURNITURE A/C.ref:NL/2

19..							
Jan 5	Cash	CB/1	250.00				

LIST OF BALANCES

	£ Debits(+)	£ Credits(-)
Capital		5,000.00
Cash	3,750.00	
Purchases	2,000.00	
R.Supple (creditor)		1,000.00
Office Furniture	250.00	
	6,000.00	6,000.00

2. A.FOOT

CAPITAL A/C.ref:GL/1

				19..			
				Mch 1	Cash	CB/1	3,000.00

CASH A/C.ref:CB/1

19..				19..			
Mch 1	Capital	CB/1	3,000.00	Mch 5	Petty Cash	PC/1	10.00
" 14	Q.Kleen	SL/1	1,000.00	" 7	Purchases	NL/1	1,000.00
				" 14	Balance	c/d	2,990.00
			4,000.00				4,000.00
Mch 15	Balance	b/d	2,990.00				

PETTY CASH A/C.ref:PC/1

19..				19..			
Mch 5	Cash	CB/1	10.00	Mch 7	Stationery	NL/3	2.00
" 13	Sales	NL/2	3.00	" 14	Balance	c/d	11.00
			13.00				13.00
Mch 15	Balance	b/d	11.00				

PURCHASES A/C.ref:NL/1

19..				19..			
Mch 7	Cash	CB/1	1,000.00				

Q.KLEEN A/C.ref:SL/1

19..				19..			
Mch 12	Sales	NL/2	1,500.00	Mch 14	Cash	CB/1	1,000.00
				" "	Balance	c/d	500.00
			1,500.00				1,500.00
Mch 15	Balance	b/d	500.00				

SALES A/C.ref:NL/2

19..				19..			
Mch 14	Balance	c/d	1,503.00	Mch 12.	Q.Kleen	SL/1	1,500.00
				" 13	Petty Cash	PC/1	3.00
			1,503.00				1,503.00
				Mch 15	Balance	b/d	1,503.00

STATIONERY A/C.ref:NL/3

19..							
Mch 7	Petty Cash	PC/1	2.00				

LIST OF BALANCES

as at 14 March 19..

		Debits(+)	Credits(-)
	£	£	£
Capital	3,000 (-)		3,000
Cash	2,990 (+)	2,990	
Petty Cash	11 (+)	11	
Purchases	1,000 (+)	1,000	
Q.Kleen (debtor)	500 (+)	500	
Sales	1,503 (-)		1,503
Stationery	2 (+)	2	
	NIL	4,503	4,503

3. (a) MONETARY POSITION AS AT 1 JANUARY 19.1:-

	£
Cash at bank and in hand	11,229
Sundry debtors	3,139
	14,368
Sundry creditors	7,421
Surplus	6,947

(b) NEW MONETARY POSITION AS AT 2 JANUARY 19.1:-

	£
Cash at bank and in hand	9,633
Sundry debtors	3,139
	12,772
Sundry creditors	5,825
Surplus	6,947

4. (a) L. MIDDLE

CASH — A/C.ref:CB/1

Date	Details	Ref	Amount	Date	Details	Ref	Amount
19..				19..			
June 1	Balance	b/d	29.00	June 8	J.Fats	PL/1	100.00
" 6	Sales	NL/2	10.00	" 15	Purchases	NL/1	25.00
" 17	"	NL/2	35.00	" 30	"	NL/1	18.00
" 19	"	NL/2	6.00	" "	Balance	c/d	41.00
" 25	M.Jonesey	SL/1	44.00				
" 27	G.Mixing	SL/2	60.00				
			184.00				184.00
July 1	Balance	b/d	41.00				

PURCHASES A/C.ref:NL/1

19..				19..			
June 2	J.Fats	PL/1	163.00	June 30.	Balance	c/d	267.00
" 4	R.Heddy	PL/2	61.00				
" 15	Cash	CB/1	25.00				
" 30	"	CB/1	18.00				
			267.00				267.00
July 1	Balance	b/d	267.00				

SALES A/C.ref:NL/2

19..				19..			
June 30	Balance	c/d	242.00	June 3	M.Jonesey	SL/1	44.00
				" 5	G.Mixing	SL/2	120.00
				" 6	Cash	CB/1	10.00
				" 14	A.Bendy	SL/3	27.00
				" 17	Cash	CB/1	35.00
				" 19	"	CB/1	6.00
			242.00				242.00
				July 1	Balance	b/d	242.00

J. FATS A/C.ref:PL/1

19..				19..			
June 8	Cash	CB/1	100.00	June 2	Purchases	NL/1	163.00
" 30	Balance	c/d	63.00				
			163.00				163.00
				July 1	Balance	b/d	63.00

R. HEDDY A/C.ref:PL/2

				19..			
				June 4	Purchases	NL/1	61.00

M. JONESEY A/C.ref:SL/1

19..				19..			
June 3	Sales	NL/2	44.00	June 25	Cash	CB/1	44.00

G. MIXING A/C.ref:SL/2

19..				19..			
June 5	Sales	NL/2	120.00	June 27	Cash	CB/1	60.00
				" 30	Balance	c/d	60.00
			120.00				120.00
July 1	Balance	b/d	60.00				

A. BENDY A/C.ref:SL/3

19..							
June 14	Sales	NL/2	27.00				

(b) DEBTORS AS AT 30 JUNE 19..

G. Mixing	60.00
A. Bendy	27.00
	£ 87.00

(c) CREDITORS AS AT 30 JUNE 19..

J. Fats	63.00
R. Heddy	61.00
	£ 124.00

(d) MONETARY POSITION AS AT 30 JUNE 19..

Cash at Bank	41
Sundry debtors	87
	128
Sundry creditors	124
Surplus	£ 4

ANSWERS TO EXERCISES

CHAPTER 4

1. CORRECTED TRIAL BALANCE AS AT 31 DECEMBER 19..

	£	£
Stock	1,000	
Cash purchases	959	
Wages	496	
Credit sales		7,600
Cash sales		26
Office furniture	470	
Sundry debtors	908	
Telephone expenses	34	
Sundry creditors		684
Capital		899
Rent and rates	242	
Credit purchases	4,291	
Cash at bank and in hand ...	809	
	9,209	9,209

2. TRIAL BALANCE AS AT 30 JUNE 19.1

		£	£
Capital	Personal		2,269
Shop fittings	Real	1,750	
Delivery vans	Real	2,024	
Purchases	Nominal	7,275	
Stationery	Nominal	51	
Rent	Nominal	700	
Cash sales	Nominal		10,235
Premises	Real	3,000	
Cash in hand	Real	223	
General expenses	Nominal	155	
Telephones	Nominal	22	
Wages	Nominal	500	
Sundry creditors	Personal		1,640
Stock 1 July 19..	Real	2,010	
Postage	Nominal	24	
Bank overdraft	Real		3,218
Credit sales	Nominal		522
Bank charges	Nominal	10	
Sundry debtors	Personal	140	
		17,884	17,884

ANSWERS TO EXERCISES

CHAPTER 5

1. See Accounting for Beginners (C. J. Dovey) pages 36–37.
2. See Accounting for Beginners (C. J. Dovey) pages 37–38.

3.

PURCHASES

19..		19..	
Jan 1 Cash	2,000.00	Jan 31 Trading Account	2,000.00

SALES

19..		19..	
Jan 31 Trading Account	2,400.00	Jan 1 Cash	2,400.00

STOCK

19..			
Jan 31 Trading Account	400.00		

TRADING ACCOUNT FOR THE MONTH ENDED 31 JAN 19..

		£			£
Purchases		2,000	Sales		2,400
Stock 31 January 19..		400			
Cost of goods sold		1,600			
Gross profit	c/d	800			
		2,400			2,400
			Gross profit	b/d	800

4. (a) CALCULATION OF STOCK ON HAND at 31 MARCH 19.1:-

	NUMBER OF UNITS				TOTAL COST
	Stock at Start	Purchases	Sales	Stock at Close	£
Articles costing 30p each	500	-	400	100	30,00
" " 25p "	-	3,000	2,000	1,000	250.00
Stock at cost 31 March 19.1				1,100	280.00

(b) Workings for Trading Account:-

			£
Stock at start	-	500 at 30p each	150
Purchases	-	3,000 at 25p each	750
Sales	-	400 at 40p each	160
		2,000 at 35p each	700
			£ 860

TRADING ACCOUNT FOR THE YEAR ENDED 31 MARCH 19.1

		£		£
Stock 1 April 19..		150	Sales	860
Purchases		750		
Goods available for sale		900		
Stock 31 March 19.1		280		
Cost of goods sold		620		
Gross profit:	c/d	240		
		860		860

(c)

STOCK

19..		19..	
Mch 31 Trading Account	150	Mch 31 Trading Account	150
19.1			
Mch 31 Trading Account	280		

5.

J. KAYNE

CAPITAL A/C.ref:GL/1

			19..		
			Oct 1 Cash	CB/1	10,000.00

CASH A/C ref: CB/1

19..			19..		
Oct 1 Capital	GL/1	10,000.00	Oct 3 Rent	NL/1	60.00
" 8 Sales	NL/2	2,300.00	" 5 Office furniture & fittings	GL/2	700.00
" 31 Balance	c/d	1,530.00	" 12 Purchases	NL/3	12,250.00
			" 25 Motor Van	GL/3	800.00
			" " Petty cash	PC/1	20.00
		13,830.00			13.830.00
			Nov 1 Balance	b/d	1,530.00

PETTY CASH A/C.ref:PC/1

19..			19..		
Oct 25 Cash	CB/1	20.00	Oct 31 General expenses	NL/4	18.00
			" " Balance	c/d	2.00
		20.00			20.00
Nov 1 Balance	b/d	2.00			

RENT A/C.ref:NL/1

19..					
Oct 3 Cash	CB/1	60.00			

OFFICE FURNITURE AND FITTINGS

A/C.ref:GL/2

19..					
Oct 5 Cash	CB/1	700.00			

SALES

A/C.ref:NL/2

19..			19..		
Oct 31 Trading Account	GL/5	11,400.00	Oct 8 Cash	CB/1	2,300.00
			" 24 S.Teeman	SL/1	9,100.00
		11,400.00			11,400.00

PURCHASES

A/C.ref:NL/3

19..			19..		
Oct 6 L. Pony	PL/1	6,000.00	Oct 31 Trading Account	GL/5	18,250.00
" 12 Cash	CB/1	12,250.00			
		18,250.00			18,250.00

L. PONY

A/C.ref:PL/1

			19..		
			Oct 6 Purchases	NL/3	6,000.00

S. TEEMAN

A/C.ref:SL/1

19..					
Oct 24 Sales	NL/2	9,100.00			

MOTOR VAN

A/C.ref:GL/3

19..					
Oct 25 Cash	CB/1	800.00			

GENERAL EXPENSES

A/C.ref:NL/4

19..					
Oct 31 Petty Cash	PC/1	18.00			

STOCK

A/C.ref:GL/4

19..					
Oct 31 Trading A/c	GL/5	11,341.00			

TRIAL BALANCE AS AT 31 OCTOBER 19..

Capital		10,000
Bank overdraft		1,530
Cash in hand	2	
Rent	60	
Office Furn & Ftgs	700	
Sales		11,400
Purchases	18,250	
L.Pony (creditor)		6,000
S.Teeman (debtor)	9,100	
Motor Van	800	
General Expenses	18	
	28,930	28,930

TRADING ACCOUNT OF J.KAYNE FOR THE MONTH ENDED 31 OCTOBER 19..

		£			£
Purchases		18,250	Sales		11,400
Stock 31 October 19..		11,341			
		6,909			
Gross profit	c/d	4,491			
		11,400			11,400
			Gross profit	b/d	4,491

6 a) L. SOOPER

TRADING ACCOUNT FOR THE YEAR ENDED 31 DECEMBER 19.1

	£	£
Sales		6,810
Stock 1 January 19.1	1,000	
Purchases	5,191	
	6,191	
Stock 31 December 19.1	921	5,270
Gross profit		1,540

b) CALCULATION OF LOSS FOR THE YEAR ENDED 31 DECEMBER 19..

Capital 1 January 19..	£1,000
Capital 1 January 19.1	800
Net loss	200

Note: the accuracy of the above calculation is dependent upon the assumption, in the absence of any information to the contrary, that during the year ended 31 December 19. . the proprietor did not withdraw any value from the business, thereby reducing the balance in the Capital Account, nor pay any additional value into the business, thereby increasing the balance in the Capital Account.

ANSWERS TO EXERCISES

CHAPTER 6

1. J. FIREMAN

TRADING AND PROFIT AND LOSS ACCOUNT FOR THE YEAR ENDED 31 DECEMBER 19..

		£			£
Purchases		15,040	Sales		16,240
Stock, 31 December 19..		1,510			
Cost of goods sold		13,530			
Gross profit	c/d	2,710			
		16,240			16,240
Rent		750	Gross profit	b/d	2,710
Light and heat		262			
General expenses		1,074			
Net profit to Capital A/c		624			
		2,710			2,710

BALANCE SHEET AS AT 31 DECEMBER 19..

	£		£	£
CAPITAL		FIXED ASSETS		
Balance, 1 January 19..	9,500	Office Furniture		1,100
Profit for the year	624	Motor Van		500
	10,124			1,500
CURRENT LIABILITIES		CURRENT ASSETS		
Sundry creditors	926	Stock	1,510	
		Sundry debtors	6,750	
		Cash at bank	1,290	9,550
	11,050			11,050

2. J. FIREMAN

TRADING AND PROFIT AND LOSS ACCOUNT FOR THE YEAR ENDED 31 DECEMBER 19.1

		£			£
Stock, 1 January 19.1		1,510	Sales		15,407
Purchases		13,450			
		14,960			
Stock, 31 December 19.1		1,953			
Cost of goods sold		13,007			
Gross profit	c/d	2,400			
		15,407			15,407
Office salaries		1,200	Gross profit	b/d	2,400
Rent		750	Net loss to Capital A/c		926
Light and heat		295			
General expenses		1,081			
		3,326			3,326

BALANCE SHEET AS AT 31 DECEMBER 19.1

	£	£		£	£
CAPITAL			**FIXED ASSETS**		
Balance 1 January 19.1		10,124	Office Furniture		1,000
Loss for the Year		926	Motor Van		500
		9,198			1,500
CURRENT LIABILITIES			**CURRENT ASSETS**		
Sundry Creditors	1,733		Stock	1,955	
Bank Overdraft	848	2,581	Sundry Debtors	8,326	10,279
		11,779			11,779

3. G. MEADOWS

TRADING AND PROFIT AND LOSS ACCOUNT FOR THE YEAR ENDED 30 JUNE 19.1

	£			£
Stock 1 July 19..	7,232	Sales		67,311
Purchases	56,900			
(goods available for sale)	64,132			
Stock 30 June 19.1	12,277			
(cost of goods sold)	51,855			
Gross profit: c/d	15,456			
	67.311			67.311
Salaries	8,009	Gross profit	b/d	15,456
Rates	164			
Light and heat	233			
Telephone expenses	182			
Postage and Stationery	105			
Sundry expenses	53			
Publicity	144			
Motor Van expenses	487			
Net profit to Capital A/c	6,079			
	15,456			15,456

BALANCE SHEET AS AT 30 JUNE 19.1

	£				£
CAPITAL		**FIXED ASSETS**			
Balance 1 July 19..	18,550	Freehold Premises			10,000
Profit for year	6,079	Office fixtures & fittings			1,400
	24,629	Motor Vans			1,500
					12,900
CURRENT LIABILITIES		**CURRENT ASSETS**			
Sundry creditors	13,405	Stock		12,277	
		Sundry debtors		11,216	
		Cash at bank	1,609		
		Cash in hand	32	1,641	25,134
	38,034				38,034

4.

PLANT AND MACHINERY

	£		£
19..			
Dec 31 Balance	6,000		

PROVISION FOR DEPRECIATION OF PLANT & MACHINERY

	£		£
		19..	
		Dec 31 Profit & Loss A/c	600

WAREHOUSE FIXTURES

	£		£
19..			
Dec 31 Balance	2,000		

PROVISION FOR DEPRECIATION OF WAREHOUSE FIXTURES

	£		£
		19..	
		Dec 31 Profit & Loss A/c	100

MOTOR VAN

	£		£
19..			
Dec 31 Balance	600		

PROVISION FOR DEPRECIATION OF MOTOR VAN

	£		£
		19..	
		Dec 31 Profit & Loss A/c	150

BALANCE SHEET AS AT 31 DECEMBER 19.. (EXTRACT)

FIXED ASSETS	£	£
Plant & Machinery at cost	6,000	
Depreciation to date	600	5,400
Warehouse Fixtures @ cost	2,000	
Depreciation to date	100	1,900
Motor Van at cost	600	
Depreciation to date	150	450
		7,750

5.

B. R. BLACKSON

BALANCE SHEET AS AT 30 SEPTEMBER 19.1

CAPITAL	£	£	FIXED ASSETS	£	£
Balance 1 October 19..		43,329	Premises at cost		30,000
Profit for year		6,425	Fixtures & Fittings @ cost	4,000	
		49,754	Depreciation to date	400	3,600
CURRENT LIABILITIES			Plant at cost	8,000	
Bank overdraft	5,028		Depreciation to date	1,000	7,000
Sundry creditors	50,000	55,028	Motor Vans at cost	4,000	
			Depreciation to date	1,000	3,000
					43,600
			CURRENT ASSETS		
			Stock	29,154	
			Sundry debtors	32,000	
			Cash in hand	28	61,182
		104,782			104,782

6. J. S. LITTLEMAN

TRADING AND PROFIT AND LOSS ACCOUNT FOR THE YEAR ENDED 31 MARCH 19.1

	£	£			£
Purchases		24,294	Sales		29,316
Stock 31 March 19.1		4,522			
(Cost of goods sold)		19,772			
Gross profit	c/d	9,544			
		29,316			29,316
Salaries		5,381	Gross profit	b/d	9,544
Rent and rates		992			
Telephone expenses		92			
Postage and stationery		104			
General expenses		77			
Vehicle running expenses		991			
Depreciation:					
Plant & Machinery	200				
Fixtures & Fittings	150				
Motor Vehicles	200	550			
Net profit to Capital		1,357			
		9,544			9,544

BALANCE SHEET AS AT 31 MARCH 19.1

	£	£		£ Cost	£ Depn	£
CAPITAL			FIXED ASSETS			
Balance 1 April 19..		1,000	Plant & Machinery	1,600	200	1,400
Profit for year		1,357	Fixtures & Fittings	1,500	150	1,350
		2,357	Motor Vehicles	1,000	200	800
				4,100	550	3,550
CURRENT LIABILITIES			CURRENT ASSETS			
Bank overdraft	7,000		Stock		4,522	
Sundry creditors	3,793	10,793	Sundry debtors		4,720	
			Cash in hand		158	9,600
		13,150				13,150

Note: Where revenue accounts and balance sheets have been produced in vertical form their accuracy can be checked from answers illustrated in double sided form.

ANSWERS TO EXERCISES

CHAPTER 7

1. (*a*) TOTAL NET ASSETS = CAPITAL LIABILITY
   (*b*) TOTAL NET ASSETS − CAPITAL LIABILITY = 0

2. See ACCOUNTING FOR BEGINNERS (C. J. Dovey) Chapter 1, page 6.

3. (*a*) & (*b*) See ACCOUNTING FOR BEGINNERS (C. J. Dovey) Chapter 1, page 4.
   (*c*) See ACCOUNTING FOR BEGINNERS (C. J. Dovey) Chapter 5, page 34.

4. (*a*) CAPITAL INVESTED is the amount which the owner of a business provides to enable the business to acquire the assets which are necessary for the operation of the business. It is calculated by totalling all value put into a business by its owner.
   (*b*) TOTAL NET ASSETS is the net worth of a business and is equal in amount to the capital liability. It is calculated by deducting from the Total Assets the total of all liabilities other than the capital liability.
   (*c*) TOTAL ASSETS consists of all the assets owned by a business irrespective of whether or not they are in possession of the business and irrespective of whether or not they have been paid for. It is calculated by totalling all the assets which are listed in the Balance Sheet.
   (*d*) CAPITAL LIABILITY is the amount which a business owes to its owner in respect of the net worth of the business, to which it is equal. It is calculated by adding profits made to capital invested and deducting therefrom withdrawals of value by the owner and losses made by the business.
   (*e*) TOTAL LIABILITIES consists of all the liabilities of a business including capital liability. It is calculated by totalling all the liabilities which are shown on the liabilities side of the traditional form of balance sheet which includes both capital liability and all other liabilities.

5. WORKING CAPITAL is the amount of the capital invested in a business remaining after the fixed assets have been paid for. It is the net Current Assets and is calculated by deducting the total CURRENT liabilities from the total CURRENT assets. The main danger from a deficiency of working capital is in the fact that there is not sufficient money circulating inwards from the current assets to satisfy the current liabilities, and the business is, therefore, falling into debt.

6. See ACCOUNTING FOR BEGINNERS (C. J. Dovey) Chapter 1, page 11.

7. (*a*) CAPITAL LIABILITY is the amount which a business owes to its owner in respect of the net worth of the business and is not intended to be met unless the business be wound up. CURRENT LIABILITIES are debts owing to persons or entities other than the owner of a business which are payable

currently, that is to say within the twelve months following the date of the Balance Sheet in which they are listed.

(*b*) See ACCOUNTING FOR BEGINNERS (C. J. Dovey) Chapter 1, page 8.

(*c*) A TRIAL BALANCE is a list of all the balances outstanding in the books of a business after all transactions which have taken place during a period of trading have been recorded therein but before the work necessary to compile the revenue accounts has been carried out. A BALANCE SHEET is a list of all the final balances outstanding in the accounts of a business at the end of a financial year after the final moves and adjustments have been made in the accounts to complete the revenue accounts.

(*d*) The total cash possessed by a business is the total of cash at bank and in hand. The NET MONETARY POSITION of a business is the net result obtained by combining the total cash possessed with the debtors and creditors. (Cash + debtors − creditors OR bank overdraft + creditors − debtors).

(*e*) See ACCOUNTING FOR BEGINNERS (C. J. Dovey) Chapter 3.

(*f*) GROSS PROFIT is the margin obtained by deducting from the selling value of goods sold and delivered to clients the cost of those goods, ignoring the cost of any goods not sold or delivered to clients and the remaining expenses of running the business. NET PROFIT is the margin remaining after all other business expenses relative to the goods sold and delivered, and to the period during which they were sold, have been deducted from the gross profit.

8. (1) Cash Book.
   (2) Petty Cash Book.
   (3) Purchases Account.
   (4) Car Expenses Account.
   (5) Stationery Account.
   (6) Light and Heat Account (or Electricity Account).

9.

DRAWINGS

19.2							
Mch 31	Balance	b/d	960.00				
" "	Purchases		15.00				
" "	Car expenses		50.00				
" "	Stationery		4.00				
" "	Electricity		13.00				

PURCHASES

19.2				19.2			
Mch 31	Balance	b/d	20,000.00	Mch 31	Drawings		15.00

SALES

19.2				19.2			
Mch 31	A. Browney		200.00	Mch 31	Balance	b/d	30,000.00

A.BROWNEY

19.2				19.2			
Mch 31	Balance	b/d	1,000.00	Mch 31	Sales (goods returned)		200.00

CAR EXPENSES

19.2				19.2			
Mch 31	Balance	b/d	150.00	Mch 31	Drawings		50.00

STATIONERY

19.2				19.2			
Mch 31	Balance	b/d	100.00	Mch 31	Drawings		4.00

ELECTRICITY

19.2				19.2			
Mch 31	Balance	b/d	170.00	Mch 31	Drawings		13.00

10.

F.SWIMMER

CAPITAL

19.3				19.3			
Dec 31	Drawings		1,666.00	Dec 31	Balance	b/d	9,155.00
" "	Balance	c/d	10,275.00	" "	Profit for year		2,786.00
			11,941.00				11,941.00
				19.4			
				Jan 1	Balance	b/d	10,275.00

DRAWINGS

19.3				19.3			
Dec 31	Car expenses		155.00	Dec 31	Capital		1,666.00
" "	Cash		1,440.00				
" "	Purchases		71.00				
			1,666.00				1,666.00

LEASEHOLD PREMISES

19.3					
Dec 31 Balance	b/d	5,000.00			

MOTOR CAR

19.3					
Dec 31 Balance	b/d	1,800.00			

STOCK

19.2			19.3		
Dec 31 Trading Account		2,364.00	Dec 31 Trading Account		2,364.00
19.3					
Dec 31 Trading Account		2,412.00			

PURCHASES

19.3			19.3		
Dec 31 Balance	b/d	20.826.00	Dec 31 Drawings		71.00
			" " Trading Account		20,755.00
		20,826.00			20,826.00

STATIONERY

19.3			19.3		
Dec 31 Balance	b/d	32.00	Dec 31 Profit & Loss A/c		32.00

SALES

19.3			19.3		
Dec 31 Trading Account		25,943.00	Dec 31 Balance	b/d	25,943.00

WAGES

19.3			19.3		
Dec 31 Balance	b/d	1,500.00	Dec 31 Profit & Loss A/c		1,500.00

RENT

19.3			19.3		
Dec 31 Balance	b/d	650.00	Dec 31 Profit & Loss A/c		650.00

LIGHT AND HEAT

19.3			19.3		
Dec 31 Balance	b/d	149.00	Dec 31 Profit & Loss A/c		149.00

FIXTURES AND FITTINGS

19.3					
Dec 31 Balance	b/d	848.00			

TELEPHONE EXPENSES

19.3			19.3		
Dec 31 Balance	b/d	35.00	Dec 31 Profit & Loss A/c		35.00

GENERAL EXPENSES

19.3			19.3		
Dec 31 Balance	b/d	62.00	Dec 31 Profit & Loss A/c		62.00

CAR EXPENSES

19.3			19.3		
Dec 31 Balance	b/d	177.00	Dec 31 Drawings		155.00
			" " Profit & Loss A/c		22.00
		177.00			177.00

CASH

19.3			19.3		
Dec 31 Balance	b/d	1,655.00	Dec 31 Drawings		1,440.00
			" " Balance	c/d	215.00
		1,655.00			1,655.00
19.4					
Jan 1 Balance	b/d	215.00			

TRIAL BALANCE 31 DECEMBER 19.3

	£	£
Capital		9,155
Drawings	1,666	
Leasehold Premises	5,000	
Motor Car	1,800	
Stock	2,364	
Purchases	20,755	
Stationery	32	
Sales		25,943
Wages	1,500	
Rent	650	
Light & Heat	149	
Fixtures & Fittings	848	
Telephone expenses	35	
General expenses	62	
Car expenses	22	
Cash at bank	215	
	35,098	35,098

TRADING AND PROFIT AND LOSS ACCOUNT FOR THE YEAR ENDED 31 DECEMBER 19.3

		£			£
Stock 1 January 19.3		2,364	Sales		25,943
Purchases		20,755			
(Goods available for sale)		23,119			
Stock 31 Dec 19.3		2,412			
(Cost of goods sold)		20,707			
Gross profit	c/d	5,236			
		25,943			25,943
Wages		1,500	Gross profit	b/d	5,236
Rent		650			
Light & Heat		149			
Telephone expenses		35			
General expenses		62			
Car expenses		22			
Stationery		32			
Net profit to Capital A/c		2,786			
		5,236			5,236

F. SWIMMER

BALANCE SHEET AS AT 31 DECEMBER 19.3

CAPITAL	£	FIXED ASSETS	£	£
Balance 1 January 19.3	9,155	Leasehold Premises		5,000
Net profit for year	2,786	Fixtures & Fittings		848
	11,941	Motor Car		1,800
Drawings	1,666			7,648
	10,275			
		CURRENT ASSETS		
		Stock	2,412	
		Cash at Bank	215	2,627
	10,275			10.275

Note: The student, in answering the above question, should have the initiative to use a drawings account but could come to a satisfactory conclusion by debiting the individual items withdrawn by the owner directly to the Capital Account.

APPENDIXES

I

LEDGER RULINGS

Ruled sheets-loose or in books or loose-leaf binders, can be obtained from stationers. Basic rulings are illustrated below:

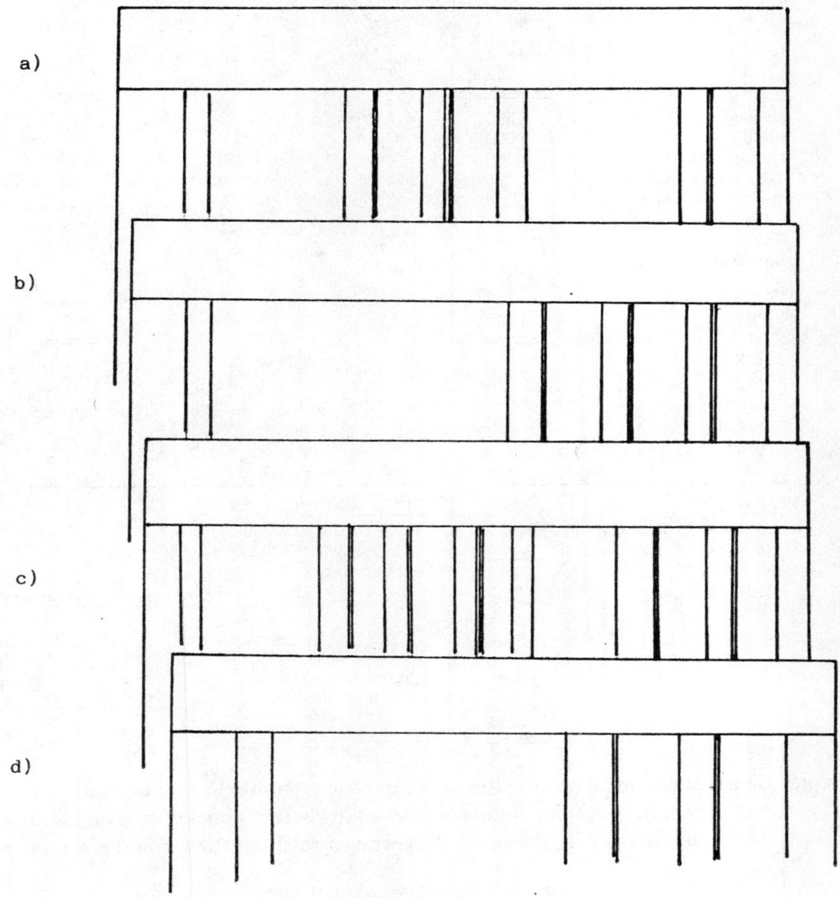

(*a*) DOUBLE LEDGER for double entry bookkeeping (Account Form).

(*b*) TREBLE CASH ANALYSIS for double entry bookkeeping in three-column form i.e. (Horizontal, Columnar or Tabular Form).

(*c*) DOUBLE CASH LEDGER for double sided balance sheets (Ignore the date and folio columns).

(*d*) DOUBLE CASH ANALYSIS for trial balances and balance sheets (Vertical Form). Ignore date and folio columns.

II

USEFUL ADDRESSES

for Information, Syllabuses and Examination Schedules

The Department of Education and Science (DES)
Elizabeth House York Road London SE1 7PH Telephone 071 934 9000

Training, Enterprise and Education Directorate
Department of Employment Moorfoot Sheffield S1 4PQ
Telephone 0742 753275

School Examinations & Assessment Council
Newcombe House 45 Notting Hill Gate London W11 3JB (For GCSE Examining Boards) Telephone 071 229 1234

Business & Technician Education Council (BTEC)
Central House Upper Woburn Place London WC1H 0HH
Telephone 071 413 8400

London Chamber of Commerce and Industry (LCCI)
69 Cannon Street London EC4N 5AB Telephone 071 248 4444

The Royal Society of Arts (RSA)
Westwood Way Coventry CV4 8HS Telephone 0203 470033

City and Guilds of London Institute
76 Portland Place London W1N 4AA Telephone 071 278 2468

Chartered Institute of Bankers (CIB) Canterbury Registrar's Department
Emmanual House Burgate Lane Canterbury Kent CT1 2XJ
Telephone 0227 762600

The Chartered Insurance Institute (CII)
31 Hillcrest Road South Woodford London E18 2JP
Telephone 081 989 8464

The Institute of Chartered Secretaries and Administrators (ICSA)
16 Park Crescent London W1N 4AH Telephone 071 580 4741

The Chartered Institute of Management Accounts (CIMA)
63/65 Portland Place London W1N 4AB Telephone 071 637 2311

The Chartered Association of Certified Accountants (CACA)
1 Woodside Place Glasgow G3 7QF Telephone 041 331 1046

The Association of Accounting Technicians (AAT)
154 Clerkenwell Road London EC1R 5AD Telephone 071 837 8600

The Institute of Financial Accountants (IFA)
Burford House 44 London Road Sevenoaks Kent TN13 1AS
Telephone 0732 458080

III

GUIDE TO INFORMATION AND ADVICE

Your local CAREERS OFFICE, listed in the Phone Book under 'CAREERS SERVICE', can inform you about FURTHER EDUCATION for YOUNG PEOPLE.

Courses in a range of academic and practical subjects are run by your local college. Ask for a prospectus.

POLYTECHNICS CENTRAL ADMISSIONS SYSTEM (PCAS), PO Box 67, Cheltenham, Gloucestershire, GL50 3SF for the location of your nearest polytechnic or college of higher education and advice on admission procedures. Ask for a leaflet. Telephone 0242 227788.

UNIVERSITY CENTRAL COUNCIL FOR ADMISSIONS (UCCA), PO Box 28, Cheltenham, Gloucestershire, GL50 3SA for information regarding University Education. Ask for a leaflet. Telephone 0242 222444.

For advice on OPEN LEARNING contact the local centre of the Training and Enterprise Council (TEC). Your local Jobcentre can give you the address and telephone number.

THE OPEN COLLEGE, Freepost TK 1006, Brentford, Middlesex, TW8 8BR can provide you with a prospectus.

If you want to START A BUSINESS contact your local Jobcentre for details of local services including the address and telephone number of the local centre of the Training and Enterprise Board (TEC). Jobcentres are listed in the Phone Book under 'EMPLOYMENT SERVICES'.

THE OPEN BUSINESS SCHOOL is the fastest growing area of the Open University. It runs a wide range of management courses including accounting and finance. Ask for the Open Business School prospectus. Customer Enquiry Service, THE OPEN UNIVERSITY, Walton Hall, Milton Keynes MK7 6AA. Telephone 0908 274066.

For information about INDUSTRY SPECIALISED TRAINING write to The National Council of Industry Training Organisations (NCITO), 5 George Lane, Royston, Hertfordshire, SG8 9AR. They can put you in touch with an appropriate ITO.

BUSINESS ENTERPRISE AGENCIES are listed in Yellow Pages.

Information regarding LOCAL ENTERPRISE AGENCIES can be obtained from BUSINESS IN THE COMMUNITY, 227a City Road, London, EC1V 1LX. Telephone 071 253 3716.

CAREER DEVELOPMENT LOANS can help individuals pay for vocational training courses lasting at least one week and up to a year. Ask at your local Jobcentre for an information booklet which includes an application form or telephone 0800 585505 free of charge.

Advice on STUDENT GRANTS can be obtained from your local Education Authority.

IV

BASIC CALCULATIONS

The answer to a calculation is its RESULT.
A whole number is an INTEGER.

Symbols

= represents the verb "EQUAL". (One and one = two)
+ represents the verb ADDITION, spoken of as "PLUS" ($1+1=2$)
− represents the verb SUBTRACTION, spoken of as "MINUS" ($2-1=1$)
× represents the verb MULTIPLICATION spoken of as "MULTIPLIED BY" ($2\times 2=4$)
÷ represents the verb DIVISION spoken of as "DIVIDED BY" ($4\div 2=2$)

Terms

SUM = the result of addition ($1+1$ results in the sum 2)
DIFFERENCE = the result of subtraction ($2-1$ results in the difference 1)
PRODUCT = the result of multiplication (2×2 results in the product of 4)
QUOTIENT = the result of division ($4\div 2$ results in the quotient 2)

Fractions

The sum of, the difference between, or the product of integers must always be another integer. The quotient of integers may be any one of the following.

(a) An integer:-

$9\div 3=3 \qquad 6\div 2=3 \qquad 4\div 2=2$

(b) A fraction:-

$1\div 4=$ one quarter $3\div 4=$ three quarters

$2\div 3=$ two thirds $8\div 9=$ eight ninths

(c) An integer and a fraction:-

$9\div 2=$ four and one half $8\div 3=$ two and two thirds

$7\div 6=$ one and a seventh $6\div 5=$ one and a fifth

A FRACTION is arrived at by division. The usual method of indicating division, alternative to the symbol previously shown, is to place a horizontal line vertically between the number to be divided and the number by which it is to be divided;-

$\frac{1}{4}=$ one quarter (one of four equal parts) $1\times\frac{1}{4}=\frac{1}{4}$

$\frac{3}{4}=$ three quarters (three of four equal parts) $3\times\frac{1}{4}=\frac{3}{4}$

$\frac{9}{2}=$ four and one half (nine halves) $9\times\frac{1}{2}=4\frac{1}{2}$

$\frac{7}{6}=$ one and one sixth (seven sixths) $7\times\frac{1}{6}=1\frac{1}{6}$

The figure denoting the number of equal parts in one integer, placed below the line is the DENOMINATOR.

The figure denoting the number of equal parts in the fraction, placed above the line, is the NUMERATOR.

Percentages

A percentage is a fraction expressed as a number of one hundredth parts:-

$$\frac{1}{100} = \text{one per cent, written as } 1\,\%$$

$$\frac{25}{100} = 25\,\% \qquad \frac{50}{100} = 50\,\% \qquad \frac{75}{100} = 75\,\%$$

To convert a fraction into a percentage, multiply the numerator by 100 and divide the result by the denominator:-

$$\frac{1}{4} = \text{per cent}\,\frac{1 \times 100}{4} = \frac{100}{4} = 25\,\%$$

$$\frac{3}{4} = \text{per cent}\,\frac{3 \times 100}{4} = \frac{300}{4} = 75\,\%$$

To find the fractional part of a given quantity, multiply by the numerator and divide by the denominator:-

$$\frac{1}{4} \text{ of } 24 = \frac{24 \times 1}{4} = \frac{24}{4} = 6$$

$$\frac{3}{4} \text{ of } 24 = \frac{24 \times 3}{4} = \frac{72}{4} = 18$$

To find a certain percentage of a given quantity, multiply by the number per cent and divide by 100:-

$$25\,\% \text{ of } 24 = \frac{24 \times 25}{100} = \frac{600}{100} = 6$$

$$75\,\% \text{ of } 24 = \frac{24 \times 75}{100} = \frac{1800}{100} = 18$$

Note that the finding of a certain fractional part or percentage of a given quantity involves multiplication:-

$$\frac{1}{4} \text{ of 24 is 24 multiplied by } \frac{1}{4}$$

$$\frac{3}{4} \text{ of 24 is 24 multiplied by } \frac{3}{4}$$

To find what fraction or percentage of a certain quantity is a different quantity necessitates division:-

$$6 \text{ as a proportion of } 24 \text{ is } 6 \div 24 = \tfrac{6}{24} = \frac{1}{4} = 25\%$$

$$18 \text{ as a proportion of } 24 \text{ is } \frac{18}{24} = \frac{3}{4} = 75\%$$

Decimals

A dot, called a POINT, is used in a number to indicate where its integer ends and its fractional part begins. In showing a fraction as a decimal, the first figure after the point denotes a number of tenths, the second figure after the point denotes a number of hundredths, the third figure a number of thousandths, and so on. The denominator is not shown but understood:-

$$1\frac{1}{10} = 1{\cdot}1 \qquad 23\frac{14}{100} = 23{\cdot}14 \qquad 357\frac{372}{1000} = 357{\cdot}372$$

$$44\frac{5758}{10{,}000} = 44{\cdot}5758$$

If there are no tenths in the decimal figure, the first figure after the point is a nought. If there are no hundredths the second figure after the point is also a nought. Should there be no thousandths the third figure would also be a nought, and so on:-

$$\text{One hundredth of one per cent} = \frac{1}{10{,}000} = {\cdot}0001 = {\cdot}01\%.$$

$$\frac{1}{1{,}000} = {\cdot}001 = {\cdot}1\%$$

$$\frac{1}{100} = {\cdot}01 = 1\%$$

$$\frac{1}{10} = {\cdot}1 = 10\%$$

$$\frac{1}{5} = {\cdot}2 = 20\%$$

$$\frac{1}{20} = {\cdot}05 = 5\%$$

$$\frac{1}{40} = {\cdot}025 = 2\frac{1}{2}\%$$

$$\frac{1}{80} = {\cdot}0125 = 1\frac{1}{4}\%$$

As many as possible common interchangeable equivalent fractions, decimals, and percentages should be committed to memory for instant recall. Examples are shown above and below.

$$\frac{1}{8} = \cdot 125 = 12\frac{1}{2}\% \quad (12\frac{1}{2} \times 8 = 100 \ \& \ 125 \times 8 = 1{,}000)$$

$$\frac{1}{4} = \cdot 25 = 25\% \quad (25 \times 4 = 100 \ \& \ 250 \times 4 = 1{,}000)$$

$$\frac{3}{8} = \cdot 375 = 37\frac{1}{2}\% \quad (375 \times 8 = 3{,}000)$$

$$\frac{1}{2} = \cdot 5 = 50\% \quad (50 \times 2 = 100)$$

$$\frac{5}{8} = \cdot 625 = 62\frac{1}{2}\% \quad (625 \times 8 = 5{,}000)$$

$$\frac{3}{4} = \cdot 75 = 75\% \quad (75 \times 4 = 300)$$

$$\frac{7}{8} = \cdot 875 = 87\frac{1}{2}\% \quad (875 \times 8 = 7{,}000)$$

The figure 0 may be described as a ZERO.

Any single figure from 0 to 9 is a DIGIT.

A method or system of calculation may be described as a PROCESS, just as a way of manufacturing or producing may be so described.

$\therefore$ = 'therefore' or 'it follows that'

To multiply by 10, move the decimal point one place to the right; to multiply by 100, move the point two places to the right; to multiply by 1,000, move it three places to the right; and so on:-

$$1{\cdot}1 \times 10 = 11 \qquad 1{\cdot}1 \times 100 = 110 \qquad 1{\cdot}1 \times 1{,}000 = 1{,}100$$

$$5{\cdot}125 \times 10 = 51{\cdot}25 \qquad 25{\cdot}6875 \times 100 = 2568{\cdot}75$$

$$375{\cdot}71875 \times 1{,}000 = 375{,}718{\cdot}75$$

Multiplication is the increasing of a number by its own value a given number of times. The number to be increased is the MULTIPLICAND. The number of times the multiplicand is to be increased is the MULTIPLIER:-

$$1{\cdot}1 \times 10 = 1{\cdot}1 + 1{\cdot}1 + 1{\cdot}1 + 1{\cdot}1 + 1{\cdot}1 + 1{\cdot}1 + 1{\cdot}1 + 1{\cdot}1 + 1{\cdot}1 + 1{\cdot}1$$

$$= 11 \text{ (The sum of } 1 \times 10 \text{ and } \cdot 1 \times 10\text{)}$$

$$3 \times 2 = 3 + 3 = 6 \text{ (3 is the multiplicand; 2 is the multiplier)}$$

$$2 \times 3 = 2+2+2 = 6 \text{ (2 is the multiplicand; 3 is the multiplier)}$$

3 and 2 or 2 and 3 are the FACTORS of the product 6

When the multiplicand is an integer, moving the decimal point to the right necessitates extending the integer by adding to it the same number of zeros as are contained in the multiplier:-

$$1 \times 10 = 10 \qquad 13 \times 100 = 1{,}300 \qquad 25 \times 1{,}000 = 25{,}000$$

To divide by any integer consisting of the digit 1 and any number of zeros, such as 10, 100 and 1,000, reverse the process described for multiplication:-

$$11 \div 10 = 1{\cdot}1 \qquad 110 \div 100 = 1{\cdot}1 \qquad 1{,}100 \div 1000 = 1{\cdot}1$$

$$\frac{51{\cdot}25}{10} = 5{\cdot}125 \qquad \frac{2568{\cdot}75}{100} = 25{\cdot}6875 \qquad \frac{375{,}718{\cdot}75}{1000} = 375{\cdot}71875$$

Division is multiplication reversed. It is the process of calculating from a product and one of its factors what must be the other factor. Alternatively, it may be described as finding the number of times one number is contained in another. When being divided by one of its factors, the product becomes the DIVIDEND. The known factor by which the dividend is to be divided, to find the quotient, becomes the DIVISOR:-

$$2 \times 3 = 6 \therefore 6 \div 3 = 2 \text{ (6 is the dividend; 3 is the divisor)}$$

$$3 \times 2 = 6 \therefore 6 \div 2 = 3 \text{ (6 is the dividend; 2 is the divisor)}$$

$$\frac{1{,}000}{8} = 125 \qquad \frac{100}{4} = 25 \qquad \frac{100}{2} = 50 \qquad \frac{100}{25} = 4$$

$$\frac{3{,}000}{8} = 375 \qquad \frac{5{,}000}{8} = 625 \qquad \frac{7{,}000}{8} = 875 \qquad \frac{7{,}000}{4} = 1750$$

If, when producing a decimal by division, a digit results which repeats itself unendingly, the digit is written only once and a point is placed over it. This is called a RECURRING DECIMAL, illustrated:-

$$\frac{1}{3} = {\cdot}\dot{3} \quad ({\cdot}333333 \text{ ad infinitum})$$

The following conversions from fraction to decimal to percentage should be memorized.

$$\frac{1}{3} = {\cdot}\dot{3} = 33\frac{1}{3}\% \qquad \frac{2}{3} = {\cdot}\dot{6} = 66\frac{2}{3}\% \qquad \frac{1}{9} = {\cdot}\dot{1} = 11{\cdot}\dot{1}\,\% \; (11\frac{1}{9}\%)$$

$$\frac{1}{6} = {\cdot}1\dot{6} = 16\frac{2}{3}\% \qquad \frac{1}{12} = {\cdot}0\dot{8} = 8\frac{1}{3}\% \qquad \frac{1}{11} = {\cdot}\dot{0}\dot{9} = 9{\cdot}\dot{0}\dot{9}\,\% \; (9\frac{1}{11}\%)$$

Where a sequence of more than one digit recurs unendingly, the point is placed over the first and last digits of the sequence:-

$$\frac{1}{7} = {\cdot}\dot{1}4285\dot{7} \quad ({\cdot}142857142857142857 \text{ ad infinitum}) \; (14\frac{2}{7}\%).$$

Adding by Accumulation

A necessary skill in adding is the ability to mentally calculate cumulative sub-totals from successive digits and successive pairs of digits:-

$$7+9 = 16;\ 16+6 = 22;\ 22+8 = 30;\ 30+5 = 35\text{: etcetera.}$$

$$7+9\ \&\ 6 = 22;\ 22+8\ \&\ 5 = 35;\ 35+3\ \&\ 4 = 42;\ \textit{etc.}$$

Of particular importance is the instant recognition of every alternative pair of digits which make a total of 10:-

1	2	3	4	5	and in reverse order	9	8	7	6
9	8	7	6	5		1	2	3	4

Alternative mental progressions in adding are illustrated:-

Digits to be added						
	↓		↓		↓	
8	8	45		45		45
7	15	37	15			37
2	17	30		30	10	
3	20	28	20		20	28
6	26	25		25		
4	30	19	30		30	19
5	35	15	35	15	35	
9	44	10		10		10
1	45	1	45		45	
		↑		↑		↑

Checks

To ensure accurate addition, every sum should be calculated in two different ways; top to bottom and bottom to top, by different progressions, or by breaking up the column into two or more sections, separately adding each section, adding the resultant sub-totals, and checking the grand total with the result obtained by another method.

INDEX